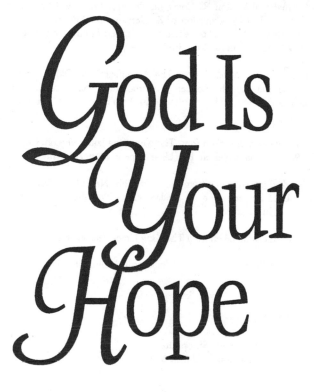

God Is Your Hope

MARIE SHROPSHIRE

HARVEST HOUSE PUBLISHERS
Eugene, Oregon 97402

Cover design by Terry Dugan Design, Minneapolis, Minnesota

GOD IS YOUR HOPE

Copyright © 1998 by Marie Shropshire
Published by Harvest House Publishers
Eugene, Oregon 97402

Library of Congress Cataloging-in-Publication Data

Shropshire, Marie, 1921–
    God is your hope / Marie Shropshire.
        p. cm.
    ISBN 1-56507-916-7
    1. Consolation. 2. Suffering—Religious aspects—Christianity—Meditations.
    3. Hope—Religious aspects—Christianity—Meditations. I. Title.
BV4905.2.S486 1999
242'.4—dc21   98-38540
                                                                        CIP

Printed in the United States of America.

99 00 01 02 03 / BC / 10 9 8 7 6 5 4 3 2

*Dedicated to my many friends
who have written to me
expressing their appreciation
for my other books
published by Harvest House.*

Contents

Hope for Your Heart

Hope for Your Heart

We can easily lose hope if we pay too much attention to the media or listen too often to people who are hurting. Or perhaps our heart is hurting because the circumstances affecting our life make it difficult for us to cling to hope. Our focus must be on God, who gives us hope. No one can live without hope.

Dr. Charles Stanley says, "Hopelessness is one of the worst feelings we can experience. Usually it comes as a result of taking our eyes off Christ and placing them on our circumstances or refusing to give Him free access to some area of our lives."

Nineteenth-century hymnwriter Edward Mote knew that God is our hope and our rock. He indicated his belief when he wrote "The Solid Rock." Let's look at his first stanza.

> *My hope is built on nothing less*
> *Than Jesus' blood and righteousness;*
> *I dare not trust the sweetest frame,*
> *But wholly lean on Jesus' name.*
> *On Christ, the solid rock, I stand;*
> *All other ground is sinking sand,*
> *All other ground is sinking sand.*

The psalmist David knew that God was his anchor, his source of hope. He wrote, "My soul faints with longing for your salvation, but I have put my hope in your word" (Psalm 119:81). Someone said, "Faith is trusting God when all human reason for hope is gone."

Peter says, "Always be prepared to give an answer to everyone who asks you to give the reason for the hope that you have" (1 Peter 3:15). Our hope lies in our assurance that Jesus died for us. And when we accept His salvation, He declares us righteous.

We can have hope because we know that God is always with us and is at work in our lives, transforming us into the likeness of His Son. Paul assures us of that when he writes, "He who began a good work in you will carry it on to completion until the day of Christ Jesus" (Philippians 1:6).

Writing on the subject "Choose Hope," Morton Kelsey says he will never forget what happened to him when a bad crisis came. "I was terribly worried. Suddenly it came to me that it was just as easy to hope as to fear. As I switched over to hoping, almost immediately new springs of life bubbled up within me, carrying me through the crisis with greater peace and strength, if not with joy. The worst finally happened, but I was so sustained that I was able to walk on through."

As you read these pages, I pray that you will be sustained so that you will be able to walk with hope through whatever comes your way.

ONE

When You're Lonely

Never will I leave you;
never will I forsake you.

—HEBREWS 13:5

⌒⌒

*D*o you ever feel as if you're standing all alone? You feel detached even when you're surrounded by people? There's an emptiness inside as if something is missing?

Those who have studied the condition of loneliness say that in spite of increased urbanization, loneliness is increasing. Loneliness is not limited to any particular group, whether age-related or otherwise; people everywhere are subject to periods of loneliness. A few years ago *Psychology Today* magazine surveyed 40,000 people and found that one of every two Americans feels lonely.

The good news is that feeling lonely is not inevitable, and it is not the end. The Lord can help you work through your lonely feelings. We need not be controlled by our feelings, but by the reliability of the Word of God.

Jesus knows the loneliness you feel. He often felt alone when He walked on the earth. He must have longed for a human touch when there was no one who thought about

His needs. Even His family thought Him strange at times. And when He needed His friends to be near Him, even His 12 most faithful followers were not always there for Him.

Moses must have been terribly lonely during his 40 years in the wilderness, with only sheep for companions. But God used those lonely times to speak to him from the burning bush. Those 40 years prepared Moses to lead the children of Israel out of Egyptian bondage.

The apostle Paul also knew what it was to feel lonely and to find his help in the Lord. He wrote to Timothy, "Do your best to come to me quickly, for Demas . . . has deserted me. . . . Only Luke is with me. . . . But the Lord stood at my side and gave me strength" (2 Timothy 4:9-11,17). Paul admitted his loneliness to his friend Timothy. It must have helped to confess his feelings; he did not deny how he felt. When you and I feel lonely, it will help if we admit our loneliness and not deny it.

When David was lonely he prayed, "Turn to me and be gracious to me, for I am lonely and afflicted" (Psalm 25:16). We can ask the Lord to fill the void that is in our hearts when we feel lonely. Loneliness is usually a condition of the heart, not an outside influence.

We can thank the Lord that He knows and understands our needs, and that He cares. It helps just to know that the Almighty One knows and cares about our every weakness and our need to feel near to someone who understands. One of our most priceless privileges is to know that God is near even when we don't feel His presence.

His eye is always upon us to protect and care for us. Everything that happens to us is for a purpose. We need not be overcome with anxiety about our feelings of loneliness. Minister/author Jack Hayford said, "Some people have found that 'flying solo' can bring the riches of solitude instead of the poverty of loneliness.

"Still, all of us, however capably we handle our lives, need people. That's why God has set the solitary in His spiritual family—to help each of us nurture and rebuild one other. Our growth and healing depend on it!"

Yet we are never really alone, even when no human friends are near. We know that God's Word is true, and we need to feel the truth of it: God is always loving and compassionate, and His peace is beyond our understanding.

God is saying to us as He said to David concerning Himself, "In the day of trouble he will keep me safe in his dwelling; he will hide me in the shelter of his tabernacle and set me high upon a rock" (Psalm 27:5).

TWO

When You're Tired of Waiting

Delight yourself in the LORD and he will give you the desires of your heart. . . . Be still before the LORD and wait patiently for him.

—PSALM 37:4,7

⌒

*M*any of us are so tired of waiting that we wonder if we'll ever be able to sing again. Our path is all uphill, and we're weary of climbing and getting nowhere. We don't want to indulge in self-pity, but we find no place to stop and rest.

We can be assured the Lord understands. There must have been times when He was here on earth that He grew tired of waiting for His people to respond to His message of love. And He must have grown tired of waiting for the time when He could return to His Father in heaven. But He waited patiently until the Father said it was time. God will never require us to wait longer than is best for us.

Let us rest in the truth of Isaiah's words: "The government will be on his shoulders" (Isaiah 9:6). All the circumstances of our life are upon our Lord. May we sense

God reaching forth to take all our cares. Isaiah further says, "Those who hope in the LORD will renew their strength. They will soar on wings like eagles; they will run and not grow weary, they will walk and not be faint" (Isaiah 40:31). When we're tired, God will renew our strength.

The people of Israel grew tired of waiting for the birth of Jesus. They knew from the prophets that Jesus was to be born, but no one knew when. There was a tremendous unrest in the world. People longed for the peace and rest which they hoped Jesus would bring.

Charles Spurgeon wrote, "The Lord always trains His soldiers, not by letting them lie on feather beds, but by turning them out . . . to hard service. . . ." That "hard service" may be a painful waiting period. The road to glory is often difficult. Spiritual growth comes about gradually and often requires periods of waiting.

The Lord can get us over those difficult roads. Charles Stanley writes, "No one else can carry you through the rough times; no one else can keep you from sinking under trials and ongoing struggles. . . . One of the things that helps in times of waiting is to [review] the promises God has given you in the past."

Elisabeth Elliot writes, "When we are puzzled by delays and detours, let us think about the great purpose of life: to glorify God."

We need to be patient and to remember that the long road leads to peace and joy. Let's wait for God as we wait for the morning. When winds of adversity are buffeting us and we're tired of waiting, we can remind ourselves that we wait not hour by hour, but minute by minute. Paul reminds us, "Be joyful in hope, patient in affliction, faithful in prayer" (Romans 12:12).

Our waiting time can cause us to lean more completely on our God. Let's stop fretting about anything over which we have no control. God is in charge. Let's rest in that knowledge and remember that God is not in a hurry.

We can know the truth spoken by the psalmist: "But you, O Lord, are a compassionate and gracious God, slow to anger, abounding in love and faithfulness" (Psalm 86:15).

How truly Annie Sherwood Hawks, a nineteenth-century hymnwriter, wrote "I Need Thee Every Hour." Her first stanza says:

> *I need Thee ev'ry hour,*
> *Most gracious Lord;*
> *No tender voice like Thine*
> *Can peace afford.*

Yes, we need Him, not only every hour but every minute of every hour. May our spiritual eyes pierce the darkness enough that we sense His presence.

God brings all His purposes to pass in His time. He has not forgotten us and our needs and desires. He is always faithful to His children.

THREE

When You're Misunderstood

The LORD upholds all those who fall
and lifts up all who are bowed down.

—PSALM 145:14

⁓

*I*t hurts so much to be misunderstood. You may feel that no one has been misunderstood or has experienced hurt or sorrow the way you have. But it may help to remember that the Lord has, and much more. He felt the pain of being misunderstood again and again during His earthly walk. He was misunderstood by His friends, His own family, and of course His enemies.

You know these painful feelings will not last forever, but sometimes you feel as if they will. You don't know what to do while you wait for things to change. It would be good if you could be like the man whom David described as one who "will have no fear of bad news; his heart is steadfast, trusting in the LORD" (Psalm 112:7). When we hear the news that we're being misunderstood, may our hearts be like the man David described—steadfast, trusting in God.

We're all different in some ways; we don't see things alike. For example, one person looks at a half-full glass and sees it as half-empty; another looks at it and says it's half-full. The latter takes the positive approach. Unless others experience life the way we do, they are likely to misunderstand us. It's difficult for them to relate to the way we behave.

We are misunderstood because we are different in our needs, motivations, perceptions, and personal values.

Each of us has a distinctive set of needs and values. Our personalities are different. Others fail to see us as we see ourselves. The better we understand that fact, the better we understand why others misunderstand us. God created each of us with a unique personality. God accepts us as we are, even if others don't. We can be grateful for that.

"Truly our behavior is complex," say Ken Voges and Ron Braund in *Understanding How Others Misunderstand You*. "Many factors affect how and why we do the things we do. One concept is clear, however: the Lord commands us to love. To seek to understand ourselves and others is to take a step toward extending to all the kind of acceptance God has extended to us."

We know that moment by moment we're kept by God's power and in God's love. Let us be thankful for that assurance and remember that His love will not let us go. He will never release His hold on us as His children. May we remember that it's not what happens to us that's most important, but our reactions to what happens.

Regardless of how much we may be misunderstood by others, God always understands us. We can affirm with the psalmist, "But you are a shield around me, O LORD; you bestow glory on me and lift up my head" (Psalm 3:3).

The Lord is our refuge today and every day. Let's dwell on His love, not on our feelings and circumstances. He will empower us to do that.

Hymnwriter D.W. Whittle found encouragement in remembering that Jesus kept him moment by moment. He tells us in his second stanza:

> Never a trial that He is not there,
> Never a burden that He doth not bear,
> Never a sorrow that He doth not share;
> Moment by moment, I'm under His care.

Jesus knows when we're burdened by the care of being misunderstood. He is present to encourage and comfort us.

As David was assured of who God is, may we say with him, "The LORD God is a sun and shield; the LORD will give grace and glory; no good thing will He withhold from those who walk uprightly" (Psalm 84:11 NKJV).

We also know the truth spoken by Isaiah the prophet: "Though the mountains be shaken and the hills be removed, yet my unfailing love for you will not be shaken nor my covenant of peace be removed" (Isaiah 54:10). Others may misunderstand us, but never our God. Why should we be disturbed about being misunderstood by anyone when we know the unfailing love of God Himself?

God loves us with an infinite love—a love that only He can give. If we look to others to supply that love, it will result only in disappointment and further misunderstanding. God always understands us fully and loves us unconditionally.

If we could only understand the depth of love God has for us, little else would matter. George Wade Robinson wrote of that love in his song "I Am His and He Is Mine."

Loved with everlasting love,
Led by grace that love to know;
Spirit, breathing from above,
Thou hast taught me it is so!
Oh, this full and perfect peace!
Oh, this transport all divine!
In a love which cannot cease,
I am His, and He is mine.

FOUR

When You're Besieged with Negative Emotions

This is the day the LORD has made;
let us rejoice and be glad in it.

—PSALM 118:24

⁓

*T*oo often we're consumed with negative thoughts—thoughts not of our own choosing. This habit pattern can affect our whole life. God's Word teaches that we are to rejoice in Him and to enjoy life. Most of us fall far short of that. We can rise above negativity by constantly replacing negative thoughts with positive thoughts.

When uninvited circumstances befall us, God knows and understands. We can draw from His strength, which never runs out. His Word says His strength is made perfect in our weakness.

Let's choose to take Christ's yoke upon ourselves and learn of Him. Then we will find the burden to be easy, as He promised. Christ has been with us in the past; He will be with us now.

Paul said, "Neither death nor life, neither angels nor demons, neither the present nor the future, nor any powers, neither height nor depth, nor anything else in all creation, will be able to separate us from the love of God that is in Christ Jesus our Lord" (Romans 8:38,39). May we grasp that truth so thoroughly that it will free us from the negative emotions that attack us.

The Lord is our Savior, and we can trust Him to be our strength and encourager when negative times hit us. Let's praise Him for His continual goodness and faithfulness to us as His children. We would do well to get into the habit of beginning each day on a positive note.

We might turn on our tape player and listen to praise music as soon as we wake up each morning. That should put our focus on the Lord, and start our day off right. Then we can discipline our emotional responses to line up for our good instead of against us.

Let's reach the point that we say with Paul, "In all these things we are more than conquerors through him who loved us" (Romans 8:37). God's desire is for us to have a good day every day by staying in a positive state of mind. We cannot have a good day any day, nor can we enjoy the peace that is ours through Jesus, as long as we're ruled by negative thoughts.

Charles Stanley writes: "God has laid the solid foundation for true peace through the cross of His Son, Jesus Christ. . . . The moment you place your trust in Christ for the forgiveness of sin, you are reconciled to God. The conflict has ended. You have been reconciled to God, who has made peace for us." A thorough grasp of that truth could set us free from negative emotions.

Sometimes we simply need to look for the silver lining in our circumstances. B.B. McKinney knew the importance of doing that. He wrote:

Though the dark clouds roll
O'er your troubled soul,
Somewhere the sun is shining;
Never doubt or fear, Christ is always near;
Look for the silver lining,
Look for the silver lining.
When the clouds are hanging low,
Always look for the silver lining,
Sweeter joys your heart will know;
Put your trust in the living Savior,
He is watching over you.
Always look for the silver lining
Till the sun comes shining through.

FIVE

When You Need a Refuge

*Let the righteous rejoice in the LORD and
take refuge in him; let all the upright
in heart praise him!*

—PSALM 64:10

⟵⟶

*A*ll of us need a place of refuge. Our tears are sometimes unceasing. Where is the refuge for the torrent of tears within us? Moses appointed cities of refuge so that an innocent person could flee there for protection from his accuser. You and I are blameless, but we may feel vulnerable and unprotected. We know that God is a more certain refuge for us than those cities were for His people in Moses' day.

We can be sure of God's faithfulness. As He was with His children of Bible times, He is with us. We must not doubt it. When the psalmist David cried out to God over and over in his times of distress, God never failed him. He always heard his plea for help. And He will hear our cry too. He is the same God as He has always been; He never changes.

Using David's words, let's pray, "In you, O LORD, I have taken refuge; let me never be put to shame. Rescue me and deliver me in your righteousness; turn your ear to me and save me. Be my rock of refuge, to which I can always go; give the command to save me, for you are my rock and my fortress" (Psalm 71:1-3).

C.B. McAfee knew that the heart of God is our place of refuge. He wrote of that in his hymn "Near to the Heart of God."

> There is a place of quiet rest,
> Near to the heart of God,
> A place where sin cannot molest,
> Near to the heart of God.
> Jesus, blest Redeemer,
> Sent from the heart of God,
> Hold us, who wait before Thee,
> Near to the heart of God.

David wrote, "He who dwells in the shelter of the Most High will rest in the shadow of the Almighty. I will say of the LORD, 'He is my refuge and my fortress, my God, in whom I trust'" (Psalm 91:1,2). We can rely on these words spoken by David.

Again David said, "Praise be to the LORD my Rock, who trains my hands for war, my fingers for battle. He is my loving God and my fortress, my stronghold and my deliverer, my shield, in whom I take refuge, who subdues peoples under me" (Psalm 144:1,2).

We know assuredly that "the salvation of the [consistently] righteous is of the LORD; He is their Refuge and secure Stronghold in the time of trouble" (Psalm 37:39 AMP), and that "God is our refuge and strength, an ever-present help in trouble" (Psalm 46:1).

We can declare with David, "My salvation and my honor depend on God; he is my mighty rock, my refuge" (Psalm 62:7). We need not let feelings of insecurity rob us of our joy. The Lord knew we would have such feelings. That's why He reminds us over and over that He is our refuge, our hiding place. God never allows us to be without such a refuge. As David declared so many times, God Himself is our refuge.

Before the psalmist repeatedly wrote of God being our refuge, the fifth book of the Bible declared, "The eternal God is your refuge, and underneath are the everlasting arms" (Deuteronomy 33:27).

SIX

When You Need Rest

Therefore my heart is glad and my tongue rejoices;
my body also will rest secure.

—PSALM 16:9

All of us grow tired—tired emotionally and physically. The circumstances of our lives weigh us down. The strain on our emotions spills over and affects our bodies. We know God is with us and that He understands, but we need to climb into His arms of love as a child climbs into his mother's lap when he is hurt.

As some of us take vacations to get away and be refreshed and enjoy scenic, restful spots, we may need to take more time each day getting away with the Lord and being spiritually refreshed. When we are sufficiently refreshed spiritually, we will experience emotional and physical refreshment.

Even as signs are erected along the highways to direct us to our vacation spots where we hope to find rest, so God has erected signs to direct us to inner places of spiritual rest. They are to be found in His presence and in His written Word.

Major Ian Thomas has this to say about spiritual vacations: "We will finally discover that the Christian life is one *vacation* after another. We are always on *vacation!* And that's *rest!* . . . not we doing nothing, but Christ doing everything in and through us. We can live relaxed as soon as we are prepared to settle for the fact that Jesus Christ is God, and that He as God is in us. God's promise of rest then becomes a reality in our lives."

Let's stop focusing on externals—worrying, trying, and striving to put into practice the Lord's admonition to "be still, and know that I am God" (Psalm 46:10). It was when Moses slowed down from his disquieting pace of life that he heard God speak from the burning bush in the desert.

The only way for you and me to be true to God and to ourselves is to be quiet and hand over all our concerns to Him. Then His strength can flow into us as the sap flows from a vine into the branches. We are branches of which the Lord is the vine. Let's cling to Him as a branch clings to its vine for sustenance.

When we fix our eyes on Christ alone, we find Him to be the fountain of our faith and our joy. Jesus invites us, "Come to me, all you who are weary and burdened, and I will give you rest. Take my yoke upon you and learn from me, for I am gentle and humble in heart, and you will find rest for your souls" (Matthew 11:28,29).

What do you think of when you think of rest? How about this definition: "Complete freedom from all anxiety"?

Paul said, "Do not be anxious about anything, but in everything, by prayer and petition, with thanksgiving, present your requests to God. And the peace of God, which transcends all understanding, will guard your hearts and your minds in Christ Jesus" (Philippians 4:6,7).

If we could allow the peace of God to "guard our hearts and minds" at all times, we would live in total rest. Joshua is an example of one who learned to live in rest.

"After the death of Moses . . . the LORD said to Joshua . . . 'Moses my servant is dead. Now then, you and all these people, get ready to cross the Jordan River into the land I am about to give to them'" (Joshua 1:1,2).

Moses had led the Israelites up *to* the land of Canaan, but no farther. Now it was the task of Joshua to lead them *into* Canaan. Canaan would be their place of rest.

This did not mean they would be free from hardships and trials. There were many battles to fight and lands to conquer. Joshua continually reminded the Israelites that the Lord would fight their battles *for* them and *through* them. They were to *rest* in God, knowing that He was in charge.

Canaan is meant to be our spiritual place of rest. But we often live below our privileges in Christ. We forget that we live in Canaan. Our life is not meant to be a wilderness experience. As with the Israelites, there are conquests to be won and spiritual battles to fight. But as God did the fighting *for* and *through* the ancient Israelites, so He wants to do with you and me.

Paul says, "Praise be to the God and Father of our Lord Jesus Christ, who has blessed us in the heavenly realms with every spiritual blessing in Christ. For he chose us in him before the creation of the world to be holy and blameless in his sight" (Ephesians 1:3,4). God chooses to bless His people. It's our responsibility to believe His Word, enter into His rest, and receive what is ours through Christ.

Peter gives us a similar word: "His divine power has given us everything we need for life and godliness through our knowledge of him who called us by his own glory and goodness. Through these he has given us his very great and precious promises, so that through them you may participate in the divine nature" (2 Peter 1:3,4).

Our anxieties disappear when we appropriate the rest that God offers.

A pastor met a 70-year-old friend at the airport one evening. He was amazed at her vitality and strength. Asked how she could walk so fast, she replied, "I don't go in my own strength. I go in the strength of the Lord." She realized her position in Christ. Drawing from His spiritual strength, she found physical strength and rest for her body. Let's affirm with the psalmist, "My salvation and my honor depend on God; he is my mighty rock, my refuge" (Psalm 62:7). A refuge is a safe place, a haven of rest.

H.L. Gilmour wrote a song about the haven of rest:

> My soul in sad exile was out on life's sea,
> So burdened with sin and distrest,
> Till I heard a sweet voice saying,
> "Make me your choice,"
> And I entered the haven of rest.
> I've anchored my soul in the haven of rest,
> I'll sail the wild seas no more.
> In Jesus I'm safe evermore.

The haven of rest is open to us anytime we're willing to enter. There are no prerequisites. We don't have to do anything to earn our way in. All we have to do is accept God's invitation.

SEVEN

When God Seems Far Away

Yet you are near, O LORD,
and all your commands are true.

—PSALM 119:151

*G*od's Word says He is always near, but sometimes we feel that He is far away. Even though we know God is always near, too often we have no *awareness* of His presence. We don't expect to live on a perpetual mountaintop; we know we can't do that. But we can ask God to enter into our seeming darkness with His freeing love, and believe that He will. We need a deeper sense of God's personal love for us. Most of us readily accept God's universal love, but that is not sufficient; we must know His *personal* love for us. We know God accepts us as we are wherever we are in our spiritual journey, and we can thank Him for that.

When the 12 spies were sent out to explore the land of Canaan, ten of them forgot that God had been with them and would continue to help them to be victorious. They saw themselves as grasshoppers. Like you and I sometimes do, they felt that God was far away.

When Joshua was chosen to take Moses' place in leading the children of Israel, the Lord said to him, "As I was with Moses, so I will be with you; I will never leave you nor forsake you. Be strong and courageous" (Joshua 1:5,6).

God never turns a deaf ear to His children who call upon Him in sincerity. The Lord spoke through Jeremiah saying, "Call to me and I will answer you and tell you great and unsearchable things you do not know" (Jeremiah 33:3). May we rest in the assurance of God's presence, knowing that we can depend on Him to answer in the time that is best. He is never far away.

Christian psychiatrist Paul Tournier said we have in the depths of our souls a secret closet whose key we have lost. Finding the key and inviting the Lord to enter that closet may be our first step toward realizing God is not far away.

When the Lord seems far away, He is allowing such feelings for a purpose. He may be teaching us to walk by faith when we are unable to sense His abiding presence. May we look only to the Lord for our joy. When we are not aware of God's presence, we may be tempted to look in other places—wrong places for fulfillment.

But we know God is our only source of satisfaction. He is the unchanging One. He is the Lord, and He never changes (see Malachi 3:6). When others fail us, He never will. His love is steadfast and unconditional. He never tires of pouring out His blessings and His mercies on His people. Hudson Taylor said, "All our difficulties are only platforms for the manifestation of His grace, power, and love."

We never have to wonder if God loves us or whether He is near. He always does. He always is. He is never at a distance. He is always beside us. We are precious to Him. As He is beside us, He also lives within us. Amazing, but true. Our relationship with God assures us that He is sensitive to our needs and desires. He doesn't even remember our past failures. He chooses to forget them.

The Bible says, "The LORD is gracious and righteous; our God is full of compassion" (Psalm 116:5). Therefore we can say with David, "My mouth will speak in praise of the LORD. Let every creature praise his holy name for ever and ever" (Psalm 145:21).

EIGHT

When Your World Looks Dark

I pray that your hearts will be flooded with light
so that you can understand the wonderful future
he has promised to those he called.

—EPHESIANS 1:18 NLT

⁓

Most of us have experienced dark times—some seem extremely dark. We may feel as if all our hopes and dreams have been dashed to nothingness. Yet we know that all is not lost, for we cannot see as God sees. But we don't have to face the darkness alone. Whether we feel it or not, we know God is with us. His love has never lessened.

Sometimes we feel guilty for our feelings. But we need not blame ourselves for being temporarily in a place of seeming darkness. Let's not carve out a rut of self-pity and revel in our darkness, but instead heed the admonition of Peter when he writes: "Casting the whole of your care [all your anxieties, all your worries, all your concerns, once and for all] on Him, for He cares for you affectionately and cares about you watchfully" (1 Peter 5:7 AMP).

Sometimes we wonder why we're required to walk through dark valleys when we long for the mountain heights where the sun shines. But our valleys are only temporary and are essential for our spiritual growth. They will not be too difficult because "[God] sends the springs into the valleys" (Psalm 104:10 NKJV).

Solomon said, "However many years a man may live, let him enjoy them all" (Ecclesiastes 11:8). When we focus on the darkness, we are refusing to find pleasure in the life God has given us to enjoy.

Paul said, "God made him [Christ] who had no sin to be sin for us, so that in him we might become the righteousness of God" (2 Corinthians 5:21). And the apostle John wrote, "God did not send his Son into the world to condemn the world, but to save the world through him" (John 3:17).

In the light of these two truths, we can be assured that we need not go on a guilt trip for feeling that our world is dark when it actually isn't. As long as we live in this world, we will experience threatening times. Strange as it seems, living life to its fullest requires times of darkness. In no other way could we know our weaknesses and our need of a Savior. We are free to enjoy life as He lives through us.

So let us embrace, not resist, the darkness. In God's time the gloom will pass and the clouds will lift. The Word tells us that "even in darkness light dawns for the upright" (Psalm 112:4). Light will dawn again, and we will understand God's purpose in having us walk through the valley. If we accept the darkness as a natural part of living, we can ward off discouragement.

Often it's in our times of darkness that God binds our hearts more closely to His. "He who began a good work in [us] will carry it on to completion until the day of Christ Jesus" (Philippians 1:6). God is in charge of our future.

He is the light in our darkness. He is our light as well as our salvation. May we say with David, "It was good for me to be afflicted so that I might learn your decrees" (Psalm 119:71). We need not fear. As we put our hands in God's and let Him lead us, we will not stumble.

David knew the source of his light. He said to the Lord, "The unfolding of your words gives light" (Psalm 119:130), and "You, O LORD, keep my lamp burning; my God turns my darkness into light" (Psalm 18:28).

We don't have to struggle to drive out the darkness. The entrance of His light dispels darkness. So all we need to do is turn on the light. "Your word is a lamp to my feet and a light for my path" (Psalm 119:105).

The Lord wastes nothing. He has a way of using every situation in our lives for good. Regardless of how dark our path may be, His love still holds us. God will allow our dark times to last only until He has accomplished His purpose within us. We know "that in all things God works for the good of those who love him, who have been called according to his purpose" (Romans 8:28). And we know that includes us.

NINE

When You've Lost a Loved One

I, even I, am he who comforts you.

—ISAIAH 51:12

⌒

We often feel unbearably alone when loved ones go to their eternal home. The clouds engulfing our souls are heavier than the ominous clouds in the sky on a dark rainy morning. We may cry with the psalmist, "In the morning, O LORD, you hear my voice; in the morning I lay my requests before you and wait in expectation" (Psalm 5:3). Our key is waiting in *expectation*, knowing that our hearts *will* be healed.

We know God is the healer of hurts, and during a time of grief we need the assurance of His comforting presence. "The LORD'S unfailing love surrounds the man who trusts in him" (Psalm 32:10). God is always with us, but we need to be brought to a place of knowing Him so well that we feel His comfort and peace even when it seems there's no hope for healing.

We can be thankful for the many passages in the Word that bring comfort to our hearts. Isaiah reminds us, "The

LORD comforts his people and will have compassion on his afflicted ones" (Isaiah 49:13). And the psalmist offers us these encouraging words: "The eyes of the LORD are on the righteous and his ears are attentive to their cry. . . . The LORD is close to the brokenhearted and saves those who are crushed in spirit" (Psalm 34:15,18).

A Scripture which we need to seek often is from the writer to the Hebrews: "[God] Himself has said, I will not in any way fail you nor give you up nor leave you without support. [I will] not, [I will] not, [I will] not in any degree leave you helpless nor forsake nor let [you] down (relax My hold on you)! [Assuredly not!]" (Hebrews 13:5 AMP).

Quoting the psalmist again: "The LORD will keep you from all harm—he will watch over your life; the LORD will watch over your coming and going both now and forevermore" (Psalm 121:7,8). Feelings of grief are perfectly normal. Our peace lies in the assurance that our heavenly Father bears our grief with us. We're not alone.

Job said, "Acquaint yourself with Him, and be at peace; thereby good will come to you" (Job 22:21 NKJV). As we acquaint ourselves more thoroughly with God, we find His peace and comfort to be sufficient. The loss of a loved one may cause us to feel that life is purposeless, but God is the foundation upon which we rebuild our lives. He is our ever-present helper. We can depend on Him at all times.

Tears are a part of our present life. Author Roger Palms writes, "That's the way things are for us now. But someday God in His tenderness will wipe away every tear, and there will be no cause for tears, because there will be no more mourning and no more pain. We all groan and suffer because of the corruption, the evil, the sin that grips this world. But someday the old will pass away. Heaven waits. That's not an empty hope or wish, but a reality."

We know the Lord suffered every grief known to man, so He is able to comfort us from His own experience. We can rest in His love. The day will come when we experience the truth expressed by John: "He will wipe every tear from their eyes. There will be no more death or mourning or crying or pain" (Revelation 21:4).

TEN

When You Feel Restless

Anyone who enters God's rest also rests from his own work, just as God did from his. Let us, therefore, make every effort to enter that rest.

—HEBREWS 4:10,11

⌒

ometimes we have to come to God asking for help with the restlessness we feel. He has freed us from feeling we have to perform a list of "shalls" and "shall-nots" in order to be acceptable to God. Yet too often there is still a lack of abiding rest in our souls. But His invitation is always open to enter His rest. Let us enter into the rest which is ours through Jesus.

Our Father's greatest desire for His children is that we simply believe in Him and trust Him in all things. But too often we're prone to rush around, trying to accomplish more than He wants us to. Let's allow Him to take away our spiritual blindness and open our eyes to see what we're doing. If we have a choice between "doing something for God" or of spending time alone with Him, He prefers the latter. It pleases Him for us to simply enjoy His presence.

Sometimes our lives get out of balance and we don't take enough time for recreation. Have you ever told yourself that you don't deserve to be happy and relaxed? Have you been so busy accomplishing things (not of God's direction) that you've felt that to be still and enjoy the beauty of life would be a waste of time? If so, you may be failing to do the things that would nourish your soul and spirit.

We can be thankful for the comfort of God's Word which we're privileged to read at any time. The psalmist said, "The LORD will command His lovingkindness in the daytime, and in the night His song shall be with me—a prayer to the God of my life" (Psalm 42:8 NKJV). However restless we may feel, God's lovingkindness is still with us. And in the night He has a song for us, just as He did for David.

God gave a song to Jean Sophia Pigott, a British composer of the nineteenth century, who learned to rest in Him "in a society that is always on the move."

JESUS, I AM RESTING, RESTING

Jesus, I am resting, resting
In the joy of what Thou art;
I am finding out the greatness
Of Thy loving heart.
Thou hast bid me gaze upon Thee,
And Thy beauty fills my soul,
For by Thy transforming power,
Thou hast made me whole.
Jesus, I am resting, resting
In the joy of what Thou art;
I am finding out the greatness
Of Thy loving heart.

When we learn to focus on God as this hymnwriter did, we too can enter the rest God intends for us. He will satisfy our heart's longings and meet our every need.

ELEVEN

When You're in Despair

Find rest, O my soul, in God alone;
my hope comes from him.

—PSALM 62:5

⟿

*S*o many things go on in our lives that can lead us to despair. We can be thankful for the privilege of sharing our feelings with God and knowing that He will understand. We don't have to pretend that everything is all right when it really isn't. Neither do we have to come to our Father with a smile on our faces when there is no smile in our hearts. He accepts and appreciates an honest heart.

Maybe we need to ask ourselves what is going on that causes our despair. One woman analyzed her situation to discover why she lived in despair. She discovered that she was overworked. She managed all the housework for a large family and could never finish all that needed doing. Dishes were in the sink and the family room was cluttered. She decided to work out a plan that would involve each family member in the chores.

Many things, both great and small, can interfere with our serenity. It may be as simple as spending too much time with gloomy people. Examining what goes on in our lives may lead to solving the problem.

Imagine the despair Moses must have felt many times as he led the 2 million Israelites out of Egypt toward the land of Canaan. Because of their disobedience and lack of faith, they spent 40 years wandering in the wilderness.

Often they complained instead of being grateful for their leader. Moses must have asked God, "How long shall I put up with these people as I lead them through this dust-laden desert and under the hot sun?" But Moses' faith led him through his feelings of despair.

God encouraged Moses as often as he needed encouragement—just as He does you and me in our times of despair. Years later, after Moses had finished his assignment and had gone on to his reward, it was recorded that there had never been a prophet in Israel like Moses.

Charles Stanley says in his little *In Touch* magazine, "There is no such thing as the life without pain and trial, and therefore no such thing as the person not in need of comfort. Don't let anyone deceive you into thinking that the key to living a joy-filled Christian life is avoiding pain—that is not possible."

Again and again the Bible tells us to praise God in every circumstance. Of course, no one feels like offering praise to God when in despair. Even though we don't feel like praising God, we can praise Him anyway, because we know who He is—a God of mercy and kindness. He will lead us out of our despondency. We never have to stay at any particular spiritual or emotional level for long. God will see to it that we continue to grow in spite of our weaknesses.

The apostle Paul said, "We are hard pressed on every side, but not crushed; perplexed, but not in despair" (2 Corinthians 4:8). The day will come when we too can say, "I am not in despair." God was Paul's hope and encourager, and He wants to be ours as well.

David spoke the truth when he said, "No one whose hope is in [God] will ever be put to shame" (Psalm 25:3). David often talked to himself and at the same time affirmed his trust in God: "He alone is my rock and my salvation; he is my fortress, I will not be shaken" (Psalm 62:6).

We bring no honor to our Savior's name as long as we are ruled by despair. Let's make Him the ruler of our lives and thoughts. We can pray with the psalmist, "May the words of my mouth and the meditation of my heart be pleasing in your sight, O LORD, my Rock and my Redeemer" (Psalm 19:14).

TWELVE

When Promises Are Delayed

I will make an everlasting covenant with them:
I will never stop doing good to them. . . .
I will rejoice in doing them good.

—JEREMIAH 32:40,41

⟋⟍

atience is not a predominant virtue for most of us. It isn't always that we doubt God's promises, but that we have difficulty keeping our eyes on Him when we have to keep waiting for a promise.

We've read of Abraham and Sarah and how they waited for many years for the fulfillment of God's promise to give them a son in their old age. Paul writes, "[For Abraham, human reason for] hope being gone, hoped in faith that he should become the father of many nations, as he had been promised. . . .

"He did not weaken in faith when he considered the [utter] impotence of his own body, which was as good as dead because he was about a hundred years old, or [when he considered] the barrenness of Sarah's [deadened] womb. No unbelief or distrust made him waver . . . but he grew strong and was empowered by faith as he gave praise and glory to

God" (Romans 4:18-20 AMP). May we exchange our doubts for that kind of faith.

Our human nature too often looks for evidence before moving out in faith. But the Word tells us that "hope that is seen is no hope at all" (Romans 8:24). Let's realize that God is our hope, and that our hopes will be fulfilled in His time.

God often works through circumstances to bring us to a place of knowing His pleasure in blessing us, whether we're receiving a promise on time or having to wait for a promise to be fulfilled.

Peter tells us, "His divine power has given us everything we need for life and godliness through our knowledge of him" (2 Peter 1:3). We know that in God's time He will indeed give us everything we need, regardless of the nature of that need. We notice that Peter says it is "through our knowledge" of God that we receive everything we need. The better we know the Lord, the more we are able to receive the blessings He intends for us.

God spoke through the prophet Isaiah and said, "Do not fear, for I am with you; do not be dismayed, for I am your God. I will strengthen you and help you; I will uphold you with my righteous right hand" (Isaiah 41:10). Those words are as true for you and me as they were for the people of Isaiah's day. We need not be afraid that God's promises will come late. He is always on time.

A troubled young woman went to talk to her pastor. Her life was full of problems and confusion. She didn't know what to do. Her pastor asked her several questions about her belief in God, to all of which she happily replied affirmatively. But she still didn't know what to do.

Then her pastor said, "If you don't know what to do, all you can do is wait and see what God will do and what He will show you. That will require patience. That doesn't mean to sit and do nothing, but to wait and watch, constantly looking to God to see what He will do. Do you believe God's desire for you in this situation is for you to be patient and trust Him?"

"Yes," she replied cheerfully, and left his office with a different look on her countenance—one of hope and peace.

In his book *Bible Readings on Hope*, Roger C. Palms writes, "When God steps into history, it is His time. You may be wishing for Him to step into your life right now. But our hope is the same as the prophets' and the shepherds' and all others who waited then. Today God asks, 'Are you ready for God's *today* in your life?'"

The psalmist said, "I wait for you, O LORD; you will answer, O Lord my God" (Psalm 38:15). We know He will answer us too. We have no reason to be doubtful concerning the fulfillment of God's promises because He is our God, the God of all hope. He is full of goodness and faithfulness.

THIRTEEN

When Your Past Haunts You

Therefore, there is now no condemnation for those who are in Christ Jesus.

—ROMANS 8:1

⌒

We realize there is nothing we can do to change our past, but if we could, there are many changes that most of us would make. We have made many mistakes we would like to undo. We know God has forgiven us, but still there is that haunting feeling that we should have done better. The Bible tells us, "If we confess our sins, he is faithful and just and will forgive us our sins and purify us from all unrighteousness" (1 John 1:9).

But we have difficulty forgiving ourselves and forgetting, not only our sins, but our little mistakes. Thoughts cling to our minds like particles of dust on the rafters in the attic. Some Christians have difficulty facing the fact that we live in a fallen, imperfect world. Because of our unfair world, we live with certain limitations.

"Much of who we are, what we do, and how we feel is determined by the past," says Christian counselor/author Norman Wright in his book *Making Peace with Your Past*. He says the memories of painful experiences that are embedded in the crevices of our mind need to be brought out and dealt with. "You don't have to be haunted by the ghosts of your past."

We need to stop being introspective and analytical of our past, constantly taking our spiritual temperature. That's God's territory. We also need to stop rehearsing unpleasant memories. God sees us as the persons we will become. We're never too weak to go to God. As we take Him our weakness, let's feel His strength. Let's see ourselves as God sees us and accept ourselves as God accepts us.

Too often we expect perfection of ourselves, but only God is perfect. Author David Seamands says, "We know that the idea of the perfect comes from a *perfect* God who created a *perfect* world with *perfect* humans made in His *perfect* image." Man was perfect before the fall in the Garden of Eden, but we lost our spiritual and emotional perfection in the fall. Some people try to atone for their sins by self-depreciation, but that only brings a sense of guilt. We are perfect only through Christ. We don't have to work at it.

"When we require perfection of ourselves, we assign our life to a set of rules," says Norman Wright. "These often come in the form of 'I must,' 'I should,' 'I ought to.' . . . But some of the urgent 'shoulds' that are born in our childhood later grow into anxious striving for today's and tomorrow's perfection."

Jesus came to free us from anything of our past that haunts us. The enemy of our souls wants to keep us in bondage to our past, but we have the power to let our past go. "God made you alive with Christ. He forgave us all our sins, having canceled the written code, with its regulations, that was against us and that stood opposed to us; he took it away, nailing it to the cross" (Colossians 2:13,14).

God sent His Son to deliver us from the prison of unhappy memories of our past. Jesus said, "The Spirit of the Lord is on me, because he has anointed me to preach good news to the poor. He has sent me to proclaim freedom for the prisoners . . . to release the oppressed, to proclaim the year of the Lord's favor" (Luke 4:18,19). We trusted in the power of the blood of the cross to save us, and that's all we need to do now. God keeps on forgiving. We don't have to give in to legalism.

Paul said, "Forgetting what is behind and straining toward what is ahead, I press on toward the goal to win the prize for which God has called me heavenward in Christ Jesus" (Philippians 3:13,14). Can we do that? With God's help we can.

Our spiritual enemy wants to keep us in bondage to everything he can. Let's stop allowing him to keep us in bondage to our past. Let's allow our past to go. We need a deeper revelation of God's personal love for us. In our quiet times let's focus more on God's love. Perhaps we need to do less praying and more listening to God's gentle, comforting voice.

Let's rejoice in God's love, and praise Him for being the forgiving God He is. David said, "[You] forgive all [my] sins and heal all [my] diseases, [You] redeem my life from the pit and crown [me] with love and compassion" (Psalm 103:3,4).

FOURTEEN

When You Feel Sorrowful

*How long must I wrestle with my thoughts
and every day have sorrow in my heart?
How long will my enemy triumph over me?*

—PSALM 13:2

We see in the above verse (and in many others) that David experienced sorrowful times. It seems that sorrow strikes at the most inopportune time, yet I suppose there is really no time that we would call opportune, for no one ever welcomes sorrow. Yet we realize that sorrow is a part of life. At one point when David felt particularly sorrowful, he asked, "How long shall I take counsel in my soul, having sorrow in my heart daily?" (Psalm 13:2 NKJV).

But David knew how to deal with his sorrows. A little later he said, "But I trust in your unfailing love; my heart rejoices in your salvation. I will sing to the LORD, for he has been good to me" (Psalm 13:5). Even as David trusted in God's unfailing love, may we learn to do the same.

Like David, I have found that songs have the power to make me feel better. And when I don't feel like singing, I can turn on my cassette player and hear spiritually uplifting songs. After a while I may find myself joining in; that's a gift from God. Someone suggested that putting our sorrows into song enables us to sing our sorrows out so they no longer bother us.

It doesn't bother God if we don't have a singing voice. He likes our voice, and He looks at our heart. That's what matters. Singing helps us to realize that regardless of what comes, we are safe because we are engulfed in God's love.

Marjorie Holmes says the more people she loses to death, the nearer she is to God. I think we could say, "The more sorrow we experience, the nearer we are to God." Scripture assures us that God is near the brokenhearted to comfort and strengthen them.

Dale Evans and Roy Rogers experienced the death of three of their children. Dale says, "Roy and I have gained the strength to endure the hard times of death because we knew God was not only near, He was with us."

In the last book of the Bible, John gives us this promise: "Now the dwelling of God is with men, and he will live with them. They will be his people, and God himself will be with them and be their God. He will wipe every tear from their eyes. There will be no more death or mourning or crying or pain" (Revelation 21:3,4). In God's strength we are able to endure life's painful times.

In her book *God in the Hard Times*, Dale Evans says, "We all have experienced the deep hurt, and, at times, bitter despair that have pressed us down so hard that we seemed to lose our ability to keep life in perspective.

"I don't believe God sends these to us, but I do believe He can provide grace that will carry us through the hard times and turn disappointments into glorious victories."

As we read our Bibles, we see how God worked in the lives of men and women who were as human as you and I. The stories in the Bible are true and never outdated. They give us insights into people that are as up-to-date as today's news stories. The same God who worked through the lives of the early-day saints is able to work today and tomorrow through us whom God calls saints. That includes you and me.

May we have our minds renewed. Let's not allow ourselves to drown in sorrow, but to see our lives and circumstances as God sees them. Let's find God's wisdom and live in the peace and comfort which He alone can give. God alone is the giver of genuine peace, comfort, and joy. He says, "I, even I, am he who comforts you" (Isaiah 51:12).

A little later He says, "[God] provides for those who grieve in Zion—to bestow on them a crown of beauty instead of ashes, the oil of gladness instead of mourning, and a garment of praise instead of a spirit of despair" (Isaiah 61:3). God does that because of His great love for us. In times of sorrow we can appropriate an extra measure of understanding of God's supreme love for us.

This doesn't mean we shouldn't give ourselves time to grieve. It may take a long time for us even to put into words the sorrow we feel. Tears are healing; let's allow them to flow as long as we need to. Many times we are totally unprepared for the death of a loved one. We're shocked. Then the pain is even greater. But we take comfort in realizing that God knows our feelings of sorrow.

Helen Steiner Rice wrote:

> There's a lot of comfort in the thought
> That sorrow, grief, and woe
> Are sent into our lives sometimes
> To help our souls to grow. . . .
> For through the depths of sorrow
> Comes understanding love,
> And peace and truth and comfort
> Are sent from God above.

You've probably heard the story of H.G. Spafford, a Chicago businessman who suffered financial disaster in the Chicago fire of 1871. His son died shortly before the fire. Spafford and his wife were still grieving over his death when they realized they needed to get away for a vacation in order to help themselves recuperate from their sorrow. His wife and four daughters went to England ahead of him. He planned to follow in a few days.

But on the Atlantic Ocean the ship was struck by another sailing vessel and sank within 12 minutes. More than 200 lives were lost, including the Spaffords' four daughters. When the survivors reached shore, Mrs. Spafford wired her husband. He booked passage on the next ship. That night Spafford penned the words to the song "It Is Well with My Soul." His first stanza reads:

> When peace like a river attendeth my way,
> When sorrows like sea billows roll;
> Whatever my lot, Thou hast taught me to say,
> "It is well, it is well with my soul."
> It is well with my soul,
> It is well, it is well with my soul.

FIFTEEN

When You Feel Hopeless

I was young and now I am old, yet I have never seen the
righteous forsaken or their children begging bread. . . . For the
Lord loves the just and will not forsake his faithful ones.

—PSALM 37:25,28

⌒

*S*ome people wake up feeling so hopeless they
don't want to get up and face the day. One
man said it is particularly painful to wake up
feeling blue because he knows that depression has spent
the night with him. One day he remembered the verse
"And now these three remain: faith, hope and love. But
the greatest of these is love" (1 Corinthians 13:13).

He realized his hopeless feelings were crowding out
faith and love. His downcast feelings were in contrast to
the truth of God. He asked himself, "Do I believe my feelings, or do I believe what God says?" He realized that God
did not create him for down times, but to trust His faith,
hope, and love.

In his book *Turn It to Gold*, Dr. James Kennedy says,
"We learn things in the midst of troubles that we do not
seem to learn any other place." He says he has heard many

people say that when they came out of affliction's furnace God spoke to them there as they had never heard Him before. Dr. Kennedy further says, "Truly we learn lessons in the darkness that we will never learn when the sun is shining brightly and all about us seems bright and peaceful."

Most of us are sometimes overwhelmed with feelings of hopelessness. We feel as if we're bogged down in a mire of desperation or trapped in a sea of hopelessness with no way out. Circumstances and situations look hopeless. Yet we know that God doesn't want us to live as if we ourselves were our only hope. Our hope must be in God, and God alone.

A turning point to spiritual growth is to learn to commit our burdens to God before they weigh us down. He stands ready to listen and respond to our cries for help. Only in Him can we find lasting hope.

Can you imagine how hopeless the three Hebrew young men must have felt when they were thrown into the fiery furnace? Or were their hope and trust so great, even at first, that they had no fear? Anyway, just as God cared for them and protected them, He will give us reason for hope too.

As we have noted previously, David had many occasions for hopelessness, but he said to the Lord, "You turned my wailing into dancing; you removed my sackcloth and clothed me with joy" (Psalm 30:11).

God says, "A righteous man may have many troubles, but the LORD delivers him from them all" (Psalm 34:19). Again He says, "Call upon me in the day of trouble; I will deliver you, and you will honor me" (Psalm 50:15).

We need real abiding hope. We know that no one can live without hope. God is a God of hope; He offers us a hope that lasts forever. And hope fills us with joy.

There is no limit to God's power. God is in control of all things as we yield ourselves to Him. His love and strength are far more powerful than any circumstance or situation we face. We need to rest in that fact and to realize that God has not forgotten us.

People everywhere have felt hopeless at times. David said, "My soul faints with longing for your salvation, but I have put my hope in your word. My eyes fail, looking for your promise; I say, 'When will you comfort me?'" (Psalm 119:81,82). Another time he talked to himself, saying, "Why are you downcast, O my soul? Why so disturbed within me? Put your hope in God, for I will yet praise him, my Savior and my God" (Psalm 42:5).

Once when David apparently was feeling strong in the Lord, he counseled, "Be strong and take heart, all you who hope in the LORD" (Psalm 31:24). You and I can have hope because we have put our trust in the Lord. We can learn to be hopeful because of Him.

Charles Stanley says, "God may be silent, but He is not idle. Therefore let this time of waiting be a place of rest. . . . One of the things that helps in times of waiting is to [review] the promises God has given you in the past."

Let's rekindle the spark of hope which He has planted within our hearts. Hope returns when we seek the Lord and adore Him with our whole hearts. Putting our trust completely in God is all we need to do. He will enable us to do that. Let's sincerely praise Him as the psalmist did.

The psalmist remembered to turn to God to lift him out of his downcast feelings. He said, "Put your hope in the LORD, for with the LORD is unfailing love" (Psalm 130:7). May we always remember that. Regardless of how dark the night may be, the sun will shine again. God never forsakes His children.

Abraham found that to be true when his faith was tested. Paul tells us, "Against all hope, Abraham in hope believed" (Romans 4:18). As Abraham believed when there was no human reason for hope, let us also believe when the odds seem to be against us. Let us learn to continually look to God in hope, and keep our hope centered in Him. May we say with the psalmist, "We wait in hope for the LORD; he is our help and our shield" (Psalm 33:20).

When we wake up with a feeling of hopelessness, we would do well to discover the reason for our feelings and then think of something to look forward to. Thinking of something we can do for others helps to get our minds off ourselves and focused on something more important.

Paul advises, "Let this mind be in you which was also in Christ Jesus" (Philippians 2:5 NKJV). Jesus never thought along the lines of hopelessness, but always of hope. Let us be challenged to follow His example. We can do it because He lives within us. He loves us and has good things planned for us every day.

Someone said, "Hope is something that miraculously comes as you let go of your anxieties and expectations and instead trust God for your tomorrows."

SIXTEEN

When You're Fearful

Be strong and courageous. Do not be afraid or
terrified . . . for the LORD your God goes with you;
he will never leave you nor forsake you.

—DEUTERONOMY 31:6

⸻

*I*n spite of all the Lord has taught us, we sometimes feel afraid. Uninvited moments of fear overtake us. Then discouragement sets in. Fear has been described as a debilitating, destructive emotion in the human heart.

You and I are not alone in our fears. Someone suggested that fear seems to be an epidemic in our society. Albert Camus, a French philosopher, called this the century of fear.

Dr. James Kennedy says, "Where faith strengthens, fear weakens. Where faith liberates, fear imprisons. Where faith empowers, fear paralyzes. Where faith encourages, fear disheartens. Where faith rejoices in its God, fear fills the heart with despair."

On their way to the Promised Land, the Israelites often allowed fear to displace their faith, and they became discouraged and disheartened. They wondered what lay ahead. At one point in their journey Moses said to them, "Do not be afraid; do not be discouraged" (Deuteronomy 1:21). Just as God was their God, He is ours. As He cared for them, He will care for us.

Our human natures are afraid of the unknown. Our future may look foreboding. We never know what circumstances are ahead. But God does, and we can trust His leadership. He says, "I guide you in the way of wisdom and lead you along straight paths. When you walk, your steps will not be hampered; when you run, you will not stumble" (Proverbs 4:11,12).

"Life doesn't always work out the way it appeared it might," says pastor Jack Hayford. "But our challenge is not to let circumstances set boundaries that seem to block our prayers and thwart our attempts to continue in the spirit of praise." God desires our praise, regardless of our circumstances. Praise helps to free us from fear.

Even though we know God will care for us, something in our frail nature causes us to be afraid of many things, and we want to shrink from them. The road ahead often looks foreboding. Perhaps it's meant to be a learning time, causing us to learn to trust God more completely. May we learn all the lessons God has planned for us. We can be thankful that God knows where He is leading us and why.

When God told Joshua that he was to take Moses' place of leadership, He knew Joshua felt anxious about his task. So God said, "Be strong and courageous. Do not be afraid or terrified . . . for the LORD your God goes with you; he will never leave you nor forsake you" (Deuteronomy 31:6). We can take God's words to Joshua as our own.

Peter wrote to those facing difficulties, "The God of all grace, who called you to his eternal glory in Christ, after you have suffered a little while, will himself restore you and make you strong, firm and steadfast" (1 Peter 5:10). We may suffer fearful times and circumstances, but God will restore us and make us strong.

Solomon wrote, "Whoso hearkens to me [Wisdom] shall dwell securely and in confident trust and shall be quiet, without fear or dread of evil" (Proverbs 1:33 AMP). Let's listen to God's wisdom and live without fear or dread.

We know we need never be afraid of God. When the Bible speaks of the fear of the Lord, it means to reverence Him and hold Him in honor and high esteem. Solomon said, "The fear of the LORD is the beginning of wisdom" (Proverbs 9:10). He meant that we are wise to acknowledge God's greatness and recognize His exalted position. To fear God in this sense is to trust Him.

Even though God is exalted on high, He looks upon His children with understanding and compassion. He understands our fears and stands ready to relieve us of them. The Word tells us, "God has not given us a spirit of fear, but of power and of love and of a sound mind" (2 Timothy 1:7 NKJV).

Sharing with God our fears, hopes, and dreams helps us to learn to trust Him more. God is never too busy to listen and answer. God loves us. Imagine the truth of these words: "The LORD your God is with you, he is mighty to save. He will take great delight in you, he will quiet you with his love, he will rejoice over you with singing" (Zephaniah 3:17). He actually delights in us, as difficult as it is for us to believe. His love is beyond our ability to understand.

When fear overtakes you, God might like to say to you, "Arise, come, my darling; my beautiful one, come with me" (Song of Solomon 2:13).

Let's accept His invitation to come away from everything that promotes fear. God is bigger than all our fears.

He longs to comfort His children and assure us of His abiding presence. In His presence is peace. Human as we are, we often find it difficult to feel God's presence. But we walk by faith, not by feelings. Again and again in His Word, God says, "Do not be afraid." Let's heed His Word and say with David, "I will fear no evil" (Psalm 23:4).

SEVENTEEN

When Your Bible Reading Seems Empty

All Scripture is God-breathed and is useful for teaching, rebuking, correcting and training in righteousness.

—2 TIMOTHY 3:16

~~~~~~~~

Most of us realize that our salvation experience was only the beginning of our walk with God. And we know that we should find joy in our Bible reading. Peter tells us, "As newborn babes, desire the pure milk of the word, that you may grow thereby" (1 Peter 2:2 NKJV).

But if our Bible reading seems as dry as the morning newspaper, we can't say that we desire the Word at all. That could mean we're not spiritually growing.

Sometimes when we read a few snatches from our Bibles, we don't take time to meditate on it. The psalmist said, "Oh, how I love your law! I meditate on it all day long" (Psalm 119:97). Most of us are not able to say that.

If we don't meditate on what we read and seek to apply it to our own life, we're hindering our spiritual growth.

Meditating on the Word, as David did, brings peace of mind, provides spiritual growth, purifies our thought life, and gives guidance to our daily lives.

The Holy Spirit can't very well guide us if we don't meditate on His Word. The Holy Spirit speaks in an inaudible voice, always in agreement with the written Word. But there's so much in the world to keep our minds earthbound instead of focused on God's Word.

The psalmist said, "I have hidden your word in my heart that I might not sin against you" (Psalm 119:11). He knew the importance of "hiding" the Word in his heart to keep from sinning. It's only through studying our Bibles and meditating on the Word that we can know Jesus. As we know Him, we better understand His Word and have a right relationship with it. Opening our hearts to the Holy Spirit frees Him to reveal the meaning of the Word to us. His Word transforms us into God's image. By the power of the Word, the Lord reshapes us to be like Himself.

As children of God, we are not all on the same path. Our levels of spiritual growth are not the same. The Lord understands that, and in His infinite love for us He meets us where we are and speaks to us on our individual level.

God's Word contains levels of truth. As we grow, we understand increasingly higher levels of truth from the Holy Word. Then the Word becomes alive and more and more meaningful to us. Most of us need a greater thirst for God and His Word. Let us learn to feed on the Word until we fall in love with it.

Eighteenth-century John Burton published a book of hymns for the children in his Sunday school. Included was the hymn "Holy Bible, Book Divine." The words of his hymn speak as much to adults as to children. Let's look at three of the stanzas.

Holy Bible, Book divine,
Precious treasure thou art mine;
Mine to tell me whence I came,
Mine to teach me what I am.

Mine to chide me when I rove,
Mine to show a Savior's love;
Mine thou art to guide and guard,
Mine to punish or reward.

Mine to tell of joys to come,
And the rebel sinner's doom;
O thou Holy Book divine,
Precious treasure, thou art mine.

EIGHTEEN

When You Feel Worthless

*You created my inmost being; you knit me
together in my mother's womb. . . . I am fearfully
and wonderfully made. . . . My frame was not
hidden from you when I was made in the secret
place. . . . All the days ordained for me were written
in your book before one of them came to be. How
precious to me are your thoughts, O God!
How vast is the sum of them!*

—PSALM 139:13-17

⌒

'm thankful that those words are written in
the Holy Word, and are as true for us today as
they were for the psalmist. They tell us that
we are valuable to God. Some of us need to read and
meditate on that truth until we no longer doubt our worth.
At the same time, let us accept our humanness.

We know we are weak and imperfect and never will be
perfect in this life. All we are and all we have comes from
God, our maker. Paul recorded that God said to him, "My
grace is sufficient for you, for my power is made perfect in
weakness" (2 Corinthians 12:9). If God's grace was sufficient for Paul, it is sufficient for you and me.

We're sometimes disappointed with ourselves. We feel unworthy. Yet we know that we are children of God because we have trusted Jesus as our personal Savior. He has adopted us and made us His very own. But we don't like the feeling of worthlessness that often plagues us. Happenings in our lives have magnified our feelings of inferiority. We may unwittingly be wearing an interior plaque bearing the word "Inferior."

Let's form a new image of ourselves and recall those times when we felt special to God. We need to relive those moments. God is as much with us to affirm us now as He has ever been. But our subconscious mind tells us that other people are more valuable in God's sight than we.

Hannah Whitall Smith, whose books have blessed the lives of many, said she went through a ten-year period of skepticism. Later she referred to that time as a time of morbid introspection. Perhaps during that time she compared herself to others, as many of us are prone to do.

In speaking of Jesus, Isaiah said, "A bruised reed he will not break, and a smoldering wick he will not snuff out" (Isaiah 42:3). You may see yourself as a bruised reed or a smoldering wick, feeling just that worthless. Jesus came to heal your brokenness and your feeling of self-dissatisfaction.

Scripture tells us we are "God's workmanship" (Ephesians 2:10). He set us apart to be a portion of His glorious inheritance (see Ephesians 1:18). Our specialness depends not on what others may say or think, not on how we see ourselves or on anything we do or fail to do, but on our relationship with the Lord. He has given us value simply because He is our Lord and Savior.

The Bible tells us that one reason Jesus came was to free those who are in bondage of any kind. That would include feelings of inferiority. Sometimes we may feel like "a smoldering wick or a bruised reed." But the Lord doesn't see us like that.

Our adversary, the devil, accuses us and wants us to see ourselves as worthless before God. But God has given us power over the enemy. Let's resist him and his accusations. As we do not have to allow a salesman to enter our house, neither do we have to allow the taunts of Satan to enter our heart or mind.

Let's heed these words of Solomon: "Keep your heart with all diligence, for out of it spring the issues of life" (Proverbs 4:23 NKJV). When we keep our hearts with all diligence, we refuse the accusations of the enemy and realize we really are precious to the Lord.

David said, "I will sing to the Lord, for he has been good to me." He has been good to you and me because He has made us His and calls us worthy. He watches over us and protects us. Paul says, "For he [God] chose us in him [Jesus] before the creation of the world to be holy and blameless in his sight" (Ephesians 1:4). If we have trusted Christ as Savior, we are "blameless in his sight." In Him we have our worth.

NINETEEN

When You're Burdened for Others

*Cast all your anxiety on him
because he cares for you.*

—1 PETER 5:7

⌒

We realize that God is our burden-bearer, but still we may find ourselves burdened down with the cares of others. We know it is a privilege to be an intercessor. But when people request prayer of us, we sometimes get too emotionally involved with their problems. We allow their problems to affect us too deeply.

Let's realize that our part is simply to agree with God, and to know that He redeems every situation. We don't need to be weighted down with care. God is in charge and cares more than any human being possibly can. Let's pray, be at peace, and leave the results with Him.

We sometimes take on more than God intended for us to. He wants us to release our prayer concerns to Him. We can let go of the pressures we feel. When we feel too much of a burden for others, we may dread coming to our prayer time.

We need to live in the truth Paul expressed to the Philippians: "Do not be anxious about anything, but in everything, by prayer and petition, with thanksgiving, present your requests to God. And the peace of God, which transcends all understanding, will guard your hearts and your minds in Christ Jesus" (Philippians 4:6,7).

The peace God gives is a kind of peace the world cannot understand. Even when our prayers are not answered in the way we hope, we can still receive the peace of God because He always knows what is best for us. Let's heed the words of the psalmist when he says, "Cast your cares on the LORD and he will sustain you; he will never let the righteous fall" (Psalm 55:22).

In prayer, as in all of life, we can trust God fully, knowing He is fulfilling His purpose. When our prayers are according to His desires, we're simply agreeing with God. We can rely on John's words with regard to prayer: "This is the confidence we have in approaching God: that if we ask anything according to his will, he hears us" (1 John 5:14). He will not fail.

Interceding for others should not rob us of our peace, but should fill us with peace, knowing we are fulfilling one of God's purposes for us. These words that Jesus spoke to His disciples apply to you and me as well: "Do not let your hearts be troubled" (John 14:1). When we refuse to let our hearts be troubled, we let go of the unnecessary burdens we bear. Every sincere prayer will be answered in God's way and in His time.

We can praise the Lord at all times and thus lift our vision above our concerns. Someone said that we acknowledge God's "above-ness" as a confession of His divine superiority. We surrender ourselves and our cares to Him.

When you've prayed a long time for an unsaved loved one with no apparent results, it may be that God is simply allowing that one to go his way for a while. God never violates a person's will. Continue praying, and wait expectantly on God. Your prayers will be answered.

We can rely on these words from Jeremiah: "This is what the LORD says: 'Restrain your voice from weeping and your eyes from tears, for your work will be rewarded,' declares the LORD. 'They will return from the land of the enemy. So there is hope for your future,' declares the LORD. Your children will return to their own land" (Jeremiah 31:16,17).

TWENTY

When You're Beset by Trials

The LORD is good and his love endures forever;
his faithfulness continues through all generations.

—PSALM 100:5

⁓

When trials come upon us, we may be tempted to doubt the goodness of God. But the psalmist was right, of course, when he proclaimed the goodness of the Lord. The Lord is indeed good, and His faithfulness never fails. God does *not* cause trials, but He does permit them. Trials are a necessary part of our spiritual development. James told us, "Consider it pure joy, my brothers, whenever you face trials of many kinds" (James 1:2).

Think what trials David had to endure before he became king of Israel. Again and again he had to flee for his life. King Saul was insanely jealous of young David. He did everything he could to take David's life. But David concluded, "The LORD is good and his love endures forever." Just as the Lord was with David, He will be with us and see us through our trials.

Robert A. Raines said in his book *To Kiss the Joy,* "So often we're blind and deaf to God's presence in our difficulties because of our own pain or anger, resentment, or self-pity. We indulge in what may be called the 'if only' syndrome . . . . Growth begins when we stop saying 'if only' and start to recognize that difficulties are opportunities to grow."

Trials can be stepping-stones to greater faith. Pastor Hayford suggests praise for dealing with trials. He says, "Praising God in the midst of difficulty stakes out God's territory over against Satan's."

When the three Hebrew young men were thrown into the fiery furnace, it is not likely that they were praising God for the fire, but for God's presence with them in the fire.

Indeed, trials are opportunities for us to grow spiritually. Jacob's favorite son, Joseph, experienced many unjust trials in his home in Canaan and later in Egypt. His trials strengthened him spiritually and prepared him for the deliverance of his own family and the whole country of Egypt from famine. Charles Stanley says there is nothing worse than a life filled with trials from which no good comes.

As I mentioned in my book *God Speaks Tenderly*, the millionaire R.G. LeTourneau could easily have paid for his four sons' college education, but he didn't. He required them to earn the money for themselves. He wanted to give them something more valuable than money—stamina to stand on their own feet, looking to their heavenly Father instead of to their earthly father. Those young men might have seen their situation as a trial, but later in life they probably appreciated their father's wisdom in the way he dealt with them.

If we focus on our trials instead of on God, we may soon find self-pity and depression to be frequent visitors. Viewing our trials from God's perspective can make us victorious. Moses, Noah, Joseph, and all the Bible heroes who endured trials were just as human as you and I. Yet they became conquerors.

Our attitude toward our trials determines whether stress or victory will result. Some people say that stress is synonymous with lack of trust. In his book *Making Stress Work for You,* Lloyd Ogilvie says, "The secret to the effective use of our God-given stress-management system . . . is somehow mysteriously linked to our relationship with God. He created us for Himself—to experience His love and power, and to love, glorify, and serve Him in response."

Jesus came to set us free from everything that hinders our spiritual growth. This includes allowing our trials to defeat us. He loves us more than our finite minds can imagine. When we abide in Him, He abides in us; and He can show us how to manage our trials so that we benefit from them instead of being overwhelmed by them.

TWENTY-ONE

When Adversity Strikes

*Dear friends, do not be surprised at the painful
trial you are suffering, as though something
strange were happening to you.*

—1 PETER 4:12

⁓

The people to whom Peter wrote the above words were probably like many Christians today. They see adversity as inconsistent with Jesus' teachings. They read words that Jesus spoke, such as, "I have come that they may have life, and that they may have it more abundantly" (John 10:10 NKJV). And questions arise in their minds.

Jesus *did* come that we might have abundant life, but to have that, we may first have to go through adversity. To isolate that Scripture from other Scriptures is to distort its meaning. We cannot understand some things that happen to us in this life, but we can trust God to somehow bring good from them. Have you read these anonymous lines?

Out of the presses of pain
Cometh the soul's best wine;
And the eyes that have shed no rain
Can shed no shine.

Whether we want to admit it or not, there's a lot of truth in that little poem. Adversity is an opportunity for God to show us His power and to bring us out stronger than we were. Until adversity hit, you did not know God's faithfulness as fully as you do now. Adversity also prepares you to be of help to others when they need you. Without adversity, our faith would not increase.

The beloved author of another century, Hannah Whitall Smith, said, "The comfort or discomfort of our inner life depends upon the dwelling place of our souls, just as the discomfort of our outward life depends largely upon the dwelling place of our bodies."

God always has a reason for allowing adversity. He knows what is best for us. We often do not recognize God's hand in our affairs until the adversity is past. But eventually we will, if we walk with Him.

Let's never be too proud to share our pain with other praying Christians. They can support us. We were never meant to bear our burdens alone. Paul writes, "Carry each other's burdens, and in this way you will fulfill the law of Christ" (Galatians 6:2).

The insightful French author Jean Guyon wrote, "Each change in your inward experience or external condition is a new test by which to try your faith and will be a help toward perfecting your soul, if you receive it with love and submission." Dale Evans Rogers suggests that we write this sentence on a card, attach it to the corner of our mirror, and read it every morning: "Mature people are not made out of good times but out of bad times."

What is a mature person? What is God up to in our lives when He allows adversity? Perhaps the best answer for both questions is found in the lives of great men and women we read about in the Bible.

God's ultimate goal is to make us like Himself. Paul tells us, "We all, with unveiled face, beholding as in a mirror the glory of the Lord, are being transformed into the same image from glory to glory" (2 Corinthians 3:18 NKJV).

We can never reach the state of sinless perfection in this life on earth, but that can be our aim. When we accept Christ as our personal Savior and Lord, the Holy Spirit creates in us potentials we never had before. It's up to us to develop, with the help of the Holy Spirit, our potential by putting into practice the truths we are being taught. As Dale Evans says, "One of the paradoxes of the Christian faith is that we learn and grow through difficulties and hard times."

The Holy Spirit was given to empower us for daily living, such as handling adversity. When we yield our lives to the power of the Spirit, we know we are growing toward spiritual maturity. We are submitted to Him. We know He is always with us, and we can talk to Him at any time. He produces in us the fruits of the Spirit—love, joy, peace, patience, kindness, goodness, faithfulness, gentleness, and self-control.

Whatever the adversity we may have to pass through, we can rely on these words of God: "When you pass through the waters, I will be with you; and when you pass through the rivers, they will not sweep over you. When you walk through the fire, you will not be burned; the flames will not set you ablaze" (Isaiah 43:2).

TWENTY-TWO

When Your Faith Is Weak

This is the victory that has overcome the world, even our faith.

—1 John 5:4

⁓

God gives us faith to trust Him on a daily basis, just as He gave us grace when we trusted Him for salvation. Paul is a wonderful example of someone who exercised great faith. Time and again he had every reason to lose his faith, but he never did.

On one occasion Paul was on a ship going to Rome with some other prisoners. He warned the officers in charge of the sailing that to continue their voyage would be dangerous because of the time of year. But they refused to listen to him. Before long the ship was caught in a severe storm.

Every man on board became fearful. To lighten the ship's load, they threw the cargo and the ship's tackle overboard. Soon everyone except Paul gave up hope of surviving. After they had gone without food for several days, Paul encouraged them. He reported that an angel had appeared to him, saying that not a life would be lost.

Paul said, "So keep up your courage, men, for I have faith in God that it will happen just as he told me" (Acts 27:25). The storm continued to rage and the ship eventually was wrecked, but no one was harmed. Paul had a conquering faith. He stood firm and God honored his faith.

Life doesn't always happen the way we expect it to. But we can accept the challenge as Paul did, and keep up our faith instead of giving up. When everything looks hopeless, God is still present. He is all-powerful and moves on behalf of His children. God stretches our faith when we go through trying circumstances.

When your faith seems small, recall past times when God delivered you. Ask Him to bring specific Scriptures to your mind—Scriptures that will help you grow in faith regarding your particular situation.

Most of our difficulties spring from a need for greater faith. One of the favorite tricks of our spiritual enemy is to use our weak faith to discourage us. How often I've fallen into that trap! I would do well to spend more time being quiet before the Lord and listening to His instruction and encouragement.

Dr. Charles Stanley suggests these seven steps for greater faith:

1. Fight the battle mentally before you step onto the battlefield.
2. Reaffirm that the battle is not yours but God's.
3. Reckon the victory even before you see it coming.
4. Wait for God's timing.
5. Fight the battle God's way, not with human ability.
6. Fight with confidence.
7. Trust God for the victory.

When our faith is weak, we might find hope by singing, or meditating on, the words of nineteenth-century Frederick Faber's hymn "Faith of Our Fathers." The first stanza reads:

> Faith of our fathers! living still
> In spite of dungeon, fire, and sword;
> O how our hearts beat high with joy
> Whene'er we hear that glorious word!
> Faith of our fathers, holy faith!
> We will be true to thee till death.

TWENTY-THREE

When You Feel Anxious

Be at rest once more, O my soul,
for the LORD has been good to you.

—PSALM 116:7

⟋⟍

*I*f we could live every moment by the admonition of the psalmist in the above verse, we would be able to let go of all anxiety. But we are frail human beings, and we allow ourselves to become anxious over many things, great and small. Ours has been called the "age of anxiety."

Paul told the Philippians not to be anxious about anything. This means we have a choice of being anxious or at rest. Rest, not anxiety, is God's will for His people. Anxiety accomplishes nothing good. It robs us of spiritual and emotional energy. God always desires what is best for us. But we have to *choose* His best.

Some people say anxiety is nothing less than unbelief in God. One proponent of this position says that to the degree we are worried about something, we are not trusting God for it. Worry robs life of the joy God means for us to have.

When Paul wrote, "Do not be anxious about any-thing," he was in a dungeon in Rome, where he was imprisoned for preaching the gospel. He was facing the prospect of a trial before Nero. Yet even in that situation he encouraged others, "Do not be anxious about anything" and "Rejoice in the Lord." Paul knew that what God was doing for him He could do for others.

Dr. James Kennedy says the cure for worry is believing God and praying to Him with a thankful heart. "Prayer is God's shock absorber for our lives." Prayer is not to be a burden, but an opportunity for refreshment. A period of daily believing prayer enables us to live in tranquility instead of in a state of anxiety. God can help us to live in serenity even in the midst of trials.

A minister told a group of friends that he was able to turn the *major* issues of his life over to God, but he had dif-ficulty with the little irritations. One of the men suggested that perhaps he was trying to handle the *little* things by himself. Whether big or little, when we try to handle any-thing without God, we fail.

You may feel sometimes as if you're the only person around who is carrying a cross. But you're not alone. Everyone has a cross to bear and the anxiety that often accompanies it. Someone said, "You have to go through Gethsemane before you can rise." Some people hide their cross behind a smile, but it's still there. Yet there is help: Jesus cares, and He will not allow us to bear our cross alone.

James tells us, "You do not have, because you do not ask God" (James 4:2). God already knows all about us, including our anxieties, but He wants us to ask Him for our specific needs. The Bible says, "Let us then approach the throne of grace with confidence, so that we may receive mercy and find grace to help us in our time of need" (Hebrews 4:16).

TWENTY-FOUR

When Your Peace Has Flown

May God himself, the God of peace, sanctify you
through and through. May your whole spirit,
soul and body be kept blameless at the
coming of our Lord Jesus Christ.

—1 THESSALONIANS 5:23

⟳

ometimes we allow our circumstances to rob
us of our peace. But the God of peace is waiting to fill us with His peace. In spite of any
turmoil you may be experiencing, you can receive an abiding peace. The peace the world offers is fleeting and shal-
low, but Jesus came to give us genuine, lasting peace
regardless of our circumstances.

Oswald Chambers wrote, "Nothing happens in any
particular [situation] unless God's will is behind it; therefore you can rest in perfect confidence in Him. Resting in
the Lord does not depend on external circumstances at all,
but on your relationship with God Himself."

Early in the life of the Israelites the Lord told Aaron to
bless the people, saying, "The LORD bless you and keep you;
the LORD make his face shine upon you and be gracious to

you; the LORD turn his face toward you and give you peace" (Numbers 6:24-26). The Lord's will always has been to bless His people with peace.

If that were not true, Paul would not have written, "Live in peace. And the God of love and peace will be with you" and "Let the peace of Christ rule in your hearts, since as members of one body you were called to peace" (2 Corinthians 13:11; Colossians 3:15).

Before the birth of Jesus the angels proclaimed a message of peace to the shepherds on the hillside: "Glory to God in the highest, and on earth peace to men on whom his favor rests" (Luke 2:14). Jesus came to bring peace to all who would receive His salvation. Yet many Christians are lacking in peace.

The more time we spend alone with the Lord, the more easily we appropriate His peace. "The LORD is good to those whose hope is in him, to the one who seeks him; it is good to wait quietly for the salvation of the LORD. . . . Let him sit alone in silence" (Lamentations 3:25,26,28). God never withholds His peace from us. He is a giving God. He never requires us to earn His peace.

Do disturbing thoughts awaken you in the night? Remind yourself that God is your peace. He is able and willing to guard your heart and mind.

Someone said he kept hoping for peace to fall on him, but it never did. He finally realized he had to bring about peace himself—with God's help, of course. Peter tells us to "turn from evil and do good . . . seek peace and pursue it" (1 Peter 3:11). According to Peter, we make a deliberate choice to receive peace. We have to "go after" it.

Solomon said, "Whoever watches the wind will not plant; whoever looks at the clouds will not reap" (Ecclesiastes 11:4). We don't just sit idly by and watch to see if peace will "fall" on us. Peace is always God's will, but we have to cooperate with Him in order to make it ours. We have to plant the seeds.

Especially in those times when we feel as if peace is a total stranger to us, we may be prone to dwell on past times when we felt completely devoid of peace. That only adds to our misery.

A man who woke up every morning feeling "down" discovered he had a habit at bedtime of reviewing all the circumstances of his life that had robbed him of peace. Finally he realized that in so doing he had invited depression to spend the night with him. As he thought about his behavior pattern, he realized he was acting in opposition to what Scripture teaches.

When he changed his bedtime habit to reading and meditating on a few verses of meaningful Scripture, his life began to change for the better. Now when melancholy feelings come upon him, he finds something in the Bible that applies to him. Then he searches his mind for something to look forward to.

The word "peace" appears more than 300 times in the Bible. When Isaiah prophesied the birth of Jesus he said, "He will be called . . . Prince of Peace" (Isaiah 9:6).

Both in the Old Testament and the New, we have promises of peace. Let's consider a few of them.

Speaking to the Lord, Isaiah said, "You will keep in perfect peace him whose mind is steadfast, because he trusts in you" (Isaiah 26:3).

The Lord said, "I will grant peace in the land, and you will lie down and no one will make you afraid" (Leviticus 26:6).

The psalmist declared, "The LORD gives strength to his people; the LORD blesses his people with peace" (Psalm 29:11).

The psalmist said to the Lord, "Great peace have they who love your law, and nothing can make them stumble" (Psalm 119:165).

Referring to the wisdom of God, Solomon said, "Her ways are pleasant ways, and all her paths are peace" (Proverbs 3:17).

Shortly before leaving this earth Jesus said, "Peace I leave with you; my peace I give you. I do not give to you as the world gives. Do not let your hearts be troubled and do not be afraid" (John 14:27).

Speaking of Jesus, Paul said, "He came and preached peace to you who were far away and peace to those who were near" (Ephesians 2:17).

If our hearts can fully grasp all these truths concerning peace, surely we will not need to say again that our peace has flown.

TWENTY-FIVE

When Circumstances Are Against You

*If God is for us,
who can be against us?*

—ROMANS 8:31

⟿

Our response to Paul's rhetorical question would be an immediate "No one, of course. God is incomparably greater than any person or circumstance could ever be." Yet it sometimes seems as if our circumstances are undeniably against us.

We live in a very real world where pain and disappointment are a part of life. Yet we forget that there is an antidote to the hard times we face. That is Jesus, our Lord. The enemy of our souls does everything he can to defeat us and cause us to give in to despair.

Peter warns us, "Be self-controlled and alert. Your enemy the devil prowls around like a roaring lion looking for someone to devour. Resist him, standing firm in the faith" (1 Peter 5:8,9).

Why does God allow the enemy to harass and trouble us? Why can't we live without so many problems? Bernard

Baruch, counselor to several United States presidents, answered that question by saying, "The art of living lies not in eliminating but in growing with troubles."

As Dale Evans Rogers said, "Mature people are not made out of good times but out of bad times." If you write those two statements on little cards and place them where you can read them every morning, your attitude can change, and you can have a new zest for life.

Jeremy Taylor, a man of the eighteenth century, said, "It is usually not so much the greatness of our trouble but the littleness of our spirit which makes us complain." We need a "greatness" of spirit to handle life when our circumstances seem to be against us.

A famous preacher told this story of his early ministry. Shortly after he went to a new location in New York City to become a pastor, a friend told him, "You sure have a tough one in that old church on Twenty-ninth Street. But if you . . . tell all who will listen that the Lord loves them and will help them if they put their trust in Him, I believe you will get results—in time."

The preacher said that those last words, "in time," proved to be true and he had to learn patience. If the Lord has given you a tough assignment, one that requires more patience than you think you have, you may think, "My circumstances are certainly against me now." That's when you need to remind yourself that God is allowing this testing time to strengthen you and to make a more mature Christian of you.

Poet Robert Browning came to a point in his life when he felt surely his circumstances were more against him than ever before. His beloved wife Elizabeth had died and his life was shattered. For three years he accomplished very little. He said he wanted to run away and hide, but he decided to make the best of his terrible circumstances.

One day Browning remembered these words from a man he greatly admired, Rabbi ben Ezra: "Approach the twilight of life with joy and hope. . . . For the last of life is the best of life. Trust God and be not afraid." That inspired Browning to write his classic poem:

> Grow old along with me!
> The best is yet to be,
> The last of life for which the first was made.
> Our times are in His hand
> Who saith: "A whole I planned."
> Youth shows but half; trust God;
> see all, nor be afraid!

TWENTY-SIX

When You Feel Guilty

Therefore, there is now no condemnation for those who are in Christ Jesus. . . . If we confess our sins, he is faithful and just and will forgive us our sins and purify us from all unrighteousness.

—ROMANS 8:1; 1 JOHN 1:9

⌒

Have you read the above words and you know you've trusted Christ, and yet you still feel guilty? If you have confessed your sin, you have no reason to feel guilty. Jesus said, "Whoever believes in him [Christ] is not condemned" (John 3:18). If we are not condemned, we are not counted as guilty. Dr. Charles Stanley says, "The major problem in handling our guilt is our misconception of God's character and nature." God is just and fair.

The Lord convicts us of our sin, so we can repent and go on our way rejoicing, knowing that we are made righteous in His sight. Have you forgiven yourself? If so, ask yourself if you have fallen for the enemy's suggestion that you're guilty. The enemy delights in making God's children miserable. Let's stop listening to his lies.

Dr. Gary Collins says in his book *Christian Counseling* that if you talk with people who have almost any problem, "You will find people who experience guilt as part of their difficulties. One writer has even suggested that guilt in some way is involved in *all* psychological problems." Some people feel guilty for feeling guilty. If you feel guilty, you're not alone.

To most Christians, the word "guilt" usually indicates sins. But the Bible seeks to make a person feel guilty *only* in order for him to repent of sin so he'll have no reason for guilt feelings. Paul explains, "Godly sorrow brings repentance that leads to salvation and leaves no regret, but worldly sorrow brings death" (2 Corinthians 7:10). Godly sorrow is constructive because it leads to helpful change. On the other hand, worldly sorrow, equivalent to guilt feelings, leads to despair.

God wants His children to move continually toward Christian maturity. But He doesn't want us to wallow in condemnation or guilt feelings. God's purpose is not to shame you, but to set you free. As an old hymn reminds us, He is the Savior of your soul.

Jesus' death on the cross paid the penalty for our sin and our guilt. We are no longer guilty. Our guilt has been washed away by the shed blood of Christ; we are justified. Peter tells us, "He himself bore our sins in his body on the tree" (1 Peter 2:24).

Our fellowship with Christ is immediately renewed when we repent and confess our sin. We need not punish ourselves. On the cross Jesus made provision for all our needs. Our sin debt has been paid in full. The desire of Jesus is to heal you. He wants to wrap you in His mercy and grace.

One writer said the preachers under whose teachings he sat in childhood made him feel guilty. They told him he disappointed God. Even now that he is saved, he hears more teaching on law than on grace. The law was given simply to make us understand our helplessness to save ourselves and bring us to Christ. We are now blameless in God's sight.

Of course, we are not perfect. We continue to sin after we're saved, but Jesus has an answer for that too. First John 2:1 says, "But if anybody does sin, we have one who speaks to the Father in our defense—Jesus Christ, the Righteous One." Because of the grace of God, we are forgiven of our future sins as well as our past sins. God's grace is so great that it is difficult for us to grasp.

Julia Johnston wrote a widely known hymn to help the doubting to experience the truth of God's grace:

Grace Greater Than Our Sin

Marvelous grace of our loving Lord,
Grace that exceeds our sin and our guilt!
Yonder on Calvary's mount outpoured—
There where the blood of the Lamb was spilt.
Grace, grace, God's grace,
Grace that will pardon and cleanse within,
Grace, grace, God's grace,
Grace that is greater than all our sin!

TWENTY-SEVEN

When You Feel Thankless

*Give thanks in all circumstances, for this is
God's will for you in Christ Jesus.*

—1 THESSALONIANS 5:18

⁓

*D*wight L. Moody told of an elderly man who gave this testimony at one of Dr. Moody's services: "I lived most of my life on Grumble Street, but after I became a Christian, I moved to Thanksgiving Street." Dr. Moody reported that the joy of gratitude made that man's face glow like the noonday sun.

One of America's greatest philosophers, Henry David Thoreau, said that every human being ought to give thanks at least once a day simply for being born. Some people whose lives have been burdensome sometimes say they wish they had never been born.

I'd like to say to that person, "If you had not been born, you would have missed feeling rain in your face, the crunch of snow under your feet, the warmth of a glowing fire on a winter evening, the song of birds, the sounds of music, the voices of friends and loved ones, and the delightful aroma of bread baking. You never would have had the thrill of overcoming a tough problem."

Several years ago about a hundred guests attended a breakfast to meet the producer of a musical which concentrated on the crucifixion and resurrection of Jesus. The producer said that prior to every performance, before the curtain went up, the cast and the stage crew gathered in a circle to thank God for the opportunity to witness of the power of Christ.

The late pastor Robert Olewiler, in whose church I had the privilege of speaking, said, "True thanksgiving is not complete until it's expressed. It must be vocal. Some people excuse themselves by saying, 'I am grateful in my heart.' That's good, but it's not completely acceptable to Jesus. Praise must be expressed."

But what if I have nothing to be thankful for? What if my circumstances go from bad to worse? Wouldn't it be hypocritical for me to express thanks when I don't feel like it? No, we are not to be guided by our feelings. We're to be obedient. Scripture tells us it's God's will to give thanks in every circumstance.

Many people have a habit of complaining when things go wrong. If that includes you and me, let's change our habit to giving thanks. Complaining never accomplishes anything. Giving thanks does. It changes our mood and outlook. It reminds us that God is in charge. He is at work in all our circumstances and will cause them to work out for our good.

Nineteenth-century preacher and teacher John A. Broadus gave several reasons for being thankful:

1. Thankfulness tends to quell complaining.
2. Thankfulness serves to soothe distress.
3. Thankfulness helps to allay anxiety.
4. Thankfulness brightens hope.
5. Thankfulness serves to strengthen us for endurance.

The psalmist said, "It is good to praise the LORD and make music to your name, O Most High, to proclaim your love in the morning and your faithfulness at night" (Psalm 92:1,2). Praising God includes expressing thanks to Him. When we go through difficulties, we can know we are still standing in the presence of God. We can choose to thank God even though we don't feel like it.

If you begin to thank God in every circumstance, you will find new hope and power. Your circumstances may not change, but you will.

The psalmist gave these thoughts concerning giving thanks:

> Make a joyful shout to the LORD, all you lands! Serve the LORD with gladness; come before His presence with singing. Know that the LORD, He is God; it is He who has made us, and not we ourselves; we are His people and the sheep of His pasture.
>
> Enter into His gates with thanksgiving, and into His courts with praise. Be thankful to Him, and bless His name. For the LORD is good; His mercy is everlasting, and His truth endures to all generations.
>
> —PSALM 100 NKJV

TWENTY-EIGHT

When You Doubt God's Love

*"Though the mountains be shaken and the hills be removed,
yet my unfailing love for you will not be shaken nor my
covenant of peace be removed," says the Lord,
who has compassion on you.*

—ISAIAH 54:10

———

*L*ove has been called the greatest thing in the world. I'm sure you and I agree. According to one concordance, the word "love" appears 493 times in the Bible. But how do I know God loves *me*—me with all my faults and shortcomings?

I can know by looking at Jesus, the Son of God, in the Bible. Hebrews 1:3 tells us, "The Son is the radiance of God's glory and the exact representation of his being." If you have read the first four books of the New Testament, you have seen again and again Jesus expressing His love, not only to the masses but to individuals. Jesus never changes. His love for you and me is as great as His love for His early followers.

God's nature is to love. He *wants* to love us because we are His creation, not because of anything we say or do to earn His love. God's love originates with Him. It will always be so.

Reading the Psalms makes it clear to me that the psalmist understood God's love more fully than most of us. He talked intimately with God, sharing his thoughts and desires with Him. One day he prayed, "Keep me as the apple of your eye" (Psalm 17:8). How much do you value the pupil of your eye? David knew that God loved him more than he treasured the pupil of his own eye.

When children are punished by their parents, they often feel there is a gross inconsistency between their love and their punishment. "How could they punish me if they love me?" they ask.

Some Christians are like that in their attitude toward God. They feel that a loving God should not allow bad things to happen to them. But as long as we live on this earth, we will experience unwanted circumstances. They have nothing to do with God's love. God's love is eternal and unchanging. As hard as it is for you to imagine, God loves you personally and individually as if you were the only person alive.

Jim Nickel tells of going with some friends to a hospital in the Philippines. They walked down the corridors singing songs about Jesus. Several young children were attracted to them. One little girl approached Jim and he reached out to her. For a few minutes he held her on his lap. Jim said he could tell she was simply starving for love. The arms of the Lord are reaching out to us just as Jim's arms reached out to the little girl. He longs to embrace us with His spiritual arms.

Minister/author Morton Kelsey says, "On the cross, Jesus did His supreme act of love. In His ascension, He ascended into heaven where He could give love out to all; and in the giving of the Spirit, He puts in every heart the capacity to respond to the love of God and reach out to others with that love.

"I have to be filled with love before love can flow through me. . . . Human attempts to love—not based on a continuous flow of divine love and not fed by springs of living water—burn out." One reason we need to know God's love is so that we can share it with others.

In her book *Pray As You Can*, Jean Gill describes God in these words:

> a God who loves us totally and unconditionally,
> just the way we are at any given moment,
> not the way we think we should be . . .
> a God who forgives us even before we realize
> we need to be forgiven . . .
> a God who wants us to be healed and whole
> and happy,
> who enjoys surprising us with lavish gifts . . .
> a God who wants to be with us in suffering
> and in joy,
> in victory and in defeat,
> in sickness and in health,
> in imprisonment and in freedom
> in death and in resurrection.*

Editor/publisher Stephen Strang says if we could just get a glimpse of how God feels about us, we would become new persons. "No matter who you are or what you've done, He longs for you to know the truth—that His affections for you are very deep, even when you are at your weakest."

God loves us and has a plan for each of us. We are precious to Him, and He sees great potential in us. Because of His love, He will help us to fulfill that potential. He is with us—always has been, always will be.

---

* © 1989 by Ave Maria Press. Reprinted with permission.

In her book *Longing for Love,* Ruth Senter thinks of the Lord saying, "I was there for you before the morning stars sang together. I am here for you when the snowstorm assaults you on the freeway. And I will be there for you when you stand before the open book. I will be there beside you when I show you what might have been. I will help you through that pain. But I also will welcome you home with 'Well done, good and faithful servant! Come and share your Master's happiness!'

"Unfailing love does not go away, even though the loved one may. Unfailing love follows close behind.

"I know about your need for visible love. Remember! I created you. I know how eagerly you look for signs, collect them and store them in your treasure box."

Paul tells, "If we are faithless, he will remain faithful, for he cannot disown himself" (2 Timothy 2:13). Regardless of how weak or faithless we may be, God still loves us and wants to show us the extent of that love. Of course, we cannot now see God's literal face, though one day we will see Him face-to-face. Only then will we be able to grasp the greatness of God's love for us. Meanwhile He continues showering His love upon us.

Samuel Francis, a hymnwriter of the nineteenth century, expressed the truth of God's love in his hymn "O the Deep, Deep Love of Jesus."

> O the deep, deep love of Jesus,
> Vast, unmeasured, boundless, free!
> Rolling as a mighty ocean
> In its fullness over me,
> Underneath me, all around me,
> Is the current of Thy love;
> Leading onward, leading homeward
> To my glorious rest above.

TWENTY-NINE

When You Feel Defeated

The Lord Almighty is with us;
the God of Jacob is our fortress.

—PSALM 46:7

⌒

To feel defeated is not a sin. Most people have felt defeated at one time or another. The important thing is not to give in to your feelings. By deciding to go on in spite of your feelings, you don't feel as defeated as you did before.

Above all, don't give up your prayer life. "You need to keep talking to God, no matter what happens, no matter how tough the world gets, no matter how furious you are. Keep talking to Him," author Beth Moore advised participants in a women's leadership conference. "The key to a healthy heart is learning to pour it out continually to God."

Author Addie Sanders asks, "How can you find blessings in defeat?" She answers, "For one thing, defeats can make you more receptive. Though Moses was raised in Egyptian luxury, life really started for him after he murdered an Egyptian foreman and ran away as a defeated man. This defeat made him more receptive to God's voice on the slopes of Sinai.

"For another thing, defeats can make you more resourceful. When a man saw the real estate he had bought in Florida sight unseen, he felt financially defeated because the land was filled with rattlesnakes. However, the defeat made him more resourceful. He opened a 'Rattlesnake Farm' and sold snake meat, skins, and even the poison!

"And for one more thing, defeats can make you more redemptive. To redeem means to set free by paying a price. When we learn how to handle defeats well, we become 'wounded healers' who become more redemptive by setting other people free from their fears and failures."

Whatever your circumstances may be, your feelings about them don't have to become a defeating way of life for you. You can climb out of your feelings. Find someone who needs a word of encouragement and spend some time giving them emotional nourishment. Start making decisions. Realize that you really do have a future. Think of ways to make it a brighter future.

Edwin Markham wrote:

> Defeat may serve as well as victory
> To shake the soul and let the glory out . . .
> Only the soul that knows the mighty grief
> Can know the mighty rapture.

In this life we will encounter situations that can lead to defeat. The well-known author Robert Louis Stevenson has been described as "on intimate terms with hard times." At one point he was so poor he couldn't pay a few dollars a month for house rent in Calistoga, California. So he prepared to take his wife and child and move to an abandoned bunkhouse. In spite of his humiliation he wrote regarding the night before leaving his house in picturesque Calistoga:

"I have never seen such a night. The sky itself was a ruddy, powerful, nameless changing color, dark and glossy like a serpent's back. The stars by innumerable millions stuck boldly forth [like] lamps. The Milky Way was bright, like a moonlit cloud; half heaven seemed Milky Way."

Stevenson refused to let defeat rule his life. Illnesses plagued him all his life. One day his wife said to him, "Robert, I don't see how you can be so happy."

Stevenson glanced at his assortment of medicine bottles lining the shelf and said, "My dear, I'm not going to let my life be regulated by a row of medicine bottles."

Feelings of defeat are often exaggerated by our thoughts of needing to be perfect. Stevenson wasn't a perfectionist. He simply had confidence in himself and in God. He apparently knew this truth expressed by Paul: "My God will meet all your needs according to his glorious riches in Christ Jesus" (Philippians 4:19).

You've probably heard that what the average patient wants is not a doctor, but an audience. Norman Elliot says in his newsletter "Release" that he finds it helpful to talk to himself. As he expresses himself verbally, anxieties drain away. If you don't have a trusted, skilled, understanding friend with whom to talk, talk to yourself about your deep feelings. Elliot says that when he talks to himself he discovers more wisdom than he thought he had.

God understands and is patient. He is ready to help you. He's waiting for you to turn to Him in prayer, Bible reading, and meditation. If you don't feel like doing any of those things, simply relax and receive from God whatever He wants you to have. Be assured that He desires only what is best for you.

THIRTY

When You Feel Needy

Are not five sparrows sold for two pennies? Yet not one of them is forgotten by God. Indeed, the very hairs of your head are all numbered. Don't be afraid; you are worth more than many sparrows.

—LUKE 12:6,7

Most of us have gone through times when we wondered how our needs would be met. Financial setbacks come, and discouragement follows. We easily forget that God has promised to supply all our needs according to His riches in glory. His storehouses are full. Yet often we are required to wait for the manifestation of His promise.

While waiting, our faith is tested. We forget God's promise to His children: "Those who seek the LORD lack no good thing" (Psalm 34:10). The psalmist also said to the Lord, "You still the hunger of those you cherish; their sons have plenty, and they store up wealth for their children" (Psalm 17:14). David probably was reminding himself of God's promise to provide more than He was reminding God.

People often ask, "Why me? Why must I suffer lack when God holds riches in store?" Much to our dismay, God often fails to answer such questions in the way we wish. He wants us to simply trust Him.

Although it may look doubtful to us, God specializes in helping those who are needy. He never fails to hear their cry for help. Our concerns are His concerns. Speaking through Isaiah, the Lord said, "For I am the LORD, your God, who takes hold of your right hand and says to you, Do not fear; I will help you" (Isaiah 41:13). The nature of our need doesn't matter, "for he will deliver the needy who cry out, the afflicted who have no one to help" (Psalm 72:12).

We may have to pass through troubled waters, but eventually the Lord will lead us to quiet streams. Speaking through Ezekiel, the Lord said, "As a shepherd looks after his scattered flock when he is with them, so will I look after my sheep" (Ezekiel 34:12). You and I are the sheep of the Lord's pasture.

Do you remember the Old Testament prophet Habakkuk? He lived in a day when times were unbelievably hard. Violence threatened the survival of his country, and it seemed as if God was doing nothing about it. But Habakkuk held onto the promise of God. He boldly declared:

> Though the fig tree does not bud
> and there are no grapes on the vines,
> though the olive crop fails
> and the fields produce no food,
> though there are no sheep in the pen
> and no cattle in the stalls,
> yet I will rejoice in the LORD,
> I will be joyful in God my Savior.
> The Sovereign LORD is my strength.
> —HABAKKUK 3:17-19

When you wonder how you will be provided for, remember that God never deserts those who follow Him. He has ways we don't know about. David said, "I was young and now I am old, yet I have never seen the righteous forsaken or their children begging bread" (Psalm 37:25).

THIRTY-ONE

When You Feel Rejected

He was despised and rejected by men,
a man of sorrows, and familiar with suffering.

—ISAIAH 53:3

〜⌒〜

*M*ost of us have felt the sting of rejection at one time or another. But none of us has experienced the pang of rejection as deeply as Jesus did. He was rejected by His own family, by His friends, and of course by His enemies.

But his greatest rejection of all came when He hung on the cross. For, the first time Jesus was cut off from His Father. "About the ninth hour Jesus cried out in a loud voice, 'Eloi, Eloi, lama sabachthani?'—which means, 'My God, my God, why have you forsaken me?'" (Matthew 27:46). That was the price He paid that we might experience salvation and acceptance.

Minister/author Derek Prince says he is convinced that one in five persons in the United States is affected in one way or another by the problem of rejection. He says even psychologists and psychiatrists acknowledge that some things are so painful that the mind refuses to focus on them. He says rejection often is "so deep, many people do not even realize their problem is rejection."

According to Dr. Prince's findings, rejection often begins in childhood and hangs on through adulthood or until healing occurs. Perhaps the best cure is for us to get at least a glimpse of how much the Father loves us. Paul tells us that God "has made us accepted in the Beloved" (Ephesians 1:6 NKJV).

Because of the price Jesus paid for our salvation, Paul was able to say also, "For I am convinced that neither death nor life, neither angels nor demons, neither the present nor the future, nor any powers, neither height nor depth, nor anything else in all creation, will be able to separate us from the love of God that is in Christ Jesus our Lord" (Romans 8:38,39).

Our spiritual enemy would like to make us feel cut off from God's love and acceptance. But he has no such power, as long as we stand against him. Let's remember that the power of Satan does not at all measure up to the power of God. John reminds us of that fact in these words: "The one who is in you is greater than the one who is in the world" (1 John 4:4).

God doesn't just tolerate us; He loves us unconditionally and accepts us just as we are. Shortly before His departure from this earth, Jesus said to His disciples, "I no longer call you servants. . . . Instead, I have called you friends" (John 15:15). He would say the same thing to us. As His children, we are special to Him.

Dr. Prince tells of meeting a woman who had a rejection problem. He was on his way to a speaking appointment and had little time for her. He said something like this to her: "Say these words after me: 'God, I thank You that You are my Father and I am Your child. Heaven is my home. I belong to the family of God. I'm not rejected. I am accepted. God loves me. He wants me. He cares for me.'"

About a month later he received a letter from the woman. She wrote, "My whole life has completely changed since I repeated those words you gave me." It may not be that simple for most of us, but when you and I feel the truth of the words the woman repeated, we'll no longer feel rejected.

The opinions of people are unimportant as long as our relationship with God is right. Let's not allow feelings of rejection to rob us of the power available to us as we trust God.

"Blessed is the man who makes the LORD his trust" (Psalm 40:4).

THIRTY-TWO

When You Can't Find God's Will

The counsel of the LORD stands forever,
The plans of His heart to all generations.

—PSALM 33:11 NKJV

⸻

nother word for *"counsel"* is *"guidance"*. A counselor is someone who advises another person. Since the counsel of the Lord stands forever, His counsel is available to you and me at all times. God does not change. He never withholds the knowledge of His will from His children. He has a plan for each of us and wants to reveal His will to us.

Would God say, "I have a plan for you," and then add, "But it's a secret. You'll have to figure it out for yourself"? Even a good earthly father wouldn't treat us like that. Jesus said, "If you, then, though you are evil, know how to give good gifts to your children, how much more will your Father in heaven give good gifts to those who ask him!" (Matthew 7:11). Good gifts include the knowledge of God's will for our lives.

Solomon said, "A wise man will hear and increase learning, and a man of understanding will attain wise counsel" (Proverbs 1:5 NKJV). As we listen to God, He increases our wisdom and we learn more and more about His will for our lives. The psalmist said, "The unfolding of your words gives light; it gives understanding to the simple" (Psalm 119:130). Even though we may be simple, God's words give us understanding.

All He asks of us is that we keep our heart sensitive to the voice of His Spirit within us. Praying and reading and meditating on God's Word helps us to discern God's will. Solomon says, "For the LORD gives wisdom, and from his mouth come knowledge and understanding" (Proverbs 2:6). That includes His showing us His will. If we tune our ears to God's wisdom, we will find His will.

The Lord told Joshua, "Do not let this Book of the Law depart from your mouth; meditate on it day and night" (Joshua 1:8). Meditating on the Word of God, especially just before we go to sleep, helps get the Word firmly into our mind, where it will bear fruit.

Counseling with godly Christians may help you clarify what God's will is for your life. Never seek counsel from a non-Christian or a very young, inexperienced person. Counsel needs to come from someone who has walked with the Lord and is spiritually mature.

The psalmist David said, "The LORD says, 'I will guide you along the best pathway for your life. I will advise you and watch over you'" (Psalm 32:8 NLT).

Another way God reveals His will is through circumstances. If you read the book of Acts, you will find such instances. For example, when Paul and his companions tried to go into Bithynia to preach, the Holy Spirit would not allow them to. He had other plans for these missionaries. If you plan to go on a particular journey, but you have no means of getting there, the Lord may be saying, "Don't go."

Several years ago I had a young friend who felt she should go to a foreign field to witness for an indefinite period of time. But she would have had to leave her husband and small child. Common sense would dictate that she should not go. God is not unreasonable or lacking in common sense.

When you feel at peace within, it is likely you are in the will of God. Sometimes individuals struggle to find God's will because they are unsure of themselves, or they are afraid of making a mistake. What are your talents? What do you enjoy doing? Does your plan fit who you are? Is it consistent with the teachings of the Bible? The answers to those questions often open the door to the knowledge of God's will.

God created us with certain abilities to be used for His glory and for our fulfillment. God desires that we find joy and satisfaction in our work. He has a wonderful plan for us. He does not often reveal the plan of a lifetime all at once, but one step at a time. Moving one step at a time teaches us to rely on God rather than on self.

Think of the happiest people you know. They are probably walking in the center of God's will, finding fulfillment in their daily work. Sometimes people look with envy on those who are fulfilled. They may think that if they imitate the person who is successful, they will be happy in the same line of work. But this may not be so. God created us uniquely. No one is exactly like you or like me. God has a unique plan for each of us.

We can expect great things from God. The psalmist said, "My soul, wait silently for God alone, for my expectation is from Him" (Psalm 62:5 NKJV). Our hope and expectation must always be in God, not in ourselves. Our intelligence, our education, our influence are nothing without God. When we have set godly goals, we can expect God to bring them to fruition.

Psychiatrist and theologian Dr. Frank Minirth says, "Because we have this powerful Person standing behind us, going before us, and ever planning the way, we have nothing to fear. There are no odds that can ultimately stop us." We may experience some tests, and we may run into some "stop signs" along the way, but in the end we will succeed.

If you have tried and failed in a certain work, it's not catastrophic. Maybe you aimed too high or too low. Try something else. Have you written down goals for your life? That should provide you with some direction. Only be sure your goals are godly ones. Will they bring glory to the kingdom of God?

Wherever you work, you are a type of minister. All of us are called to minister spontaneously wherever we are. Paul tells us, "Set your minds on things above, not on earthly things" (Colossians 3:2). In other words, we labor not simply for earthly gain, but to let the light of God shine through us in the midst of our work.

"May he give you the desire of your heart and make all your plans succeed" (Psalm 20:4).

THIRTY-THREE

When You Lack Fulfillment

However many years a man may live,
let him enjoy them all.

—ECCLESIASTES 11:8

⟶

*O*ur Creator and heavenly Father desires that His children be happy and fulfilled. Something obviously is wrong if we lack fulfillment and joy. Life is meant to be enjoyed. Sadly, some people look for enjoyment in the wrong places. The theme of Ecclesiastes is "Everything is meaningless apart from God." There is no fulfillment outside of the Lord.

Today I received a letter from an unhappy young man who has tried all kinds of worldly things, looking for fulfillment and contentment. He has given up his ungodly life, and he knows God has forgiven him, but he is having to pay the consequences for his sinful past. Right now he is unable to follow Paul's admonition to "rejoice in the Lord always" (Philippians 4:4).

John tells us, "If the Son sets you free, you will be free indeed" (John 8:36). If you lack fulfillment, you are not as free as you can be. Are you bound by a prison of dissatisfaction, ideas, and opinions? The prison of lack of fulfillment is a type of bondage keeping you from being satisfied. But it's a prison you can escape from.

One reason for lack of fulfillment is our unawareness of God's wonderful love. Are you seeking to earn God's love? You can't earn it. He loves you just as you are. We're not on a performance-based acceptance standard. After we accept the Lord's salvation, we are His beloved children. We need to see ourselves through God's eyes—loved and accepted as we are.

I read recently that the majority of our hospital beds are occupied by mental patients, and that the solution to their problems is to experience genuine love. A person cannot be fulfilled unless he feels loved. And, of course, only God can offer real, genuine, unconditional love. If I did not know that love, I would be an unfulfilled person.

If you feel unfulfilled, ask yourself, "What would I have to do or be in order to feel fulfilled?" From the time I was a child, I wanted to write. After teaching school for 28 years, I began to write. I've never felt so complete and fulfilled as I have since becoming a published author.

A certain minister left the pastorate because he could not deal with his lack of success and the church's lack of growth. Perhaps the Lord had not called him to be a pastor. Soon he began writing Christian articles and poems. He found that no amount of editors' rejection slips could discourage him. He became a successful author, knowing that the Lord had always meant for him to find fulfillment not in pastoring a church but in writing.

Whatever you pursue, you may have to make some sacrifices before you arrive. Most people do. Don't let that discourage you if you feel you are in the Lord's chosen place for you.

Successful author Louis L'Amour said, "People don't wear out; they give up. As far as trails go, there's always an open trail for the mind if you keep the doors wide open and give it a chance." Let's never feel that we are helpless victims who will never find fulfillment.

Solomon gave excellent advice when he said, "Commit to the LORD whatever you do, and your plans will succeed" (Proverbs 16:3).

THIRTY-FOUR

When You Need Encouragement

Be strong and courageous.

—JOSHUA 1:6

⌒

When we think of hope, most of us tend to think in terms of our future. But hope is for both now and eternity. God provides hope, comfort, and encouragement to us at all times. He is always aware of our needs and circumstances. He knows we cannot survive without hope.

David wrote, "The eyes of the LORD are on those . . . whose hope is in his unfailing love" (Psalm 33:18).

"The great characteristic of the Christian life is that we live in hope," says Minnete Drumwright. "Peter wrote his letter called the 'gospel of hope' to give encouragement and instruction to believers struggling to cope with the hardships of daily life. . . . Christian hope sustains us in the midst of vulnerabilities, for hope is born out of complete confidence, belief, and trust in the resurrected Christ."

If you've read the book of Psalms, you have noticed how David almost continually looked to God for hope and encouragement. At one point in his life he said, "My soul faints with longing for your salvation, but I have put my hope in your word" (Psalm 119:81). David knew God was his anchor, his source of hope and encouragement.

Peter says, "Always be prepared to give an answer to everyone who asks you to give the reason for the hope that you have" (1 Peter 3:15). Our hope rests in the fact that Jesus died and rose again for us. When we accept His salvation, He declares us righteous. Our identity is in Him.

We can be encouraged because we know God is always with us and is at work in us, transforming us into the likeness of His Son. Paul assures us of this when he writes, "He who began a good work in you will carry it on to completion until the day of Christ Jesus" (Philippians 1:6).

God is always ready to give us hope and encouragement. Paul writes, "May our Lord Jesus Christ himself and God our Father, who loved us and by his grace gave us eternal encouragement and good hope, encourage your hearts and strengthen you in every good deed and word" (2 Thessalonians 2:16,17).

The writer to the Hebrews says, "We have this hope as an anchor for the soul, firm and secure" (Hebrews 6:19). All God's promises and all His blessings are for us simply because we are His children.

Sometimes hope seems fragile or distant. We may be tempted to wonder if God has forgotten us. But we can have our hope anchored in Christ even in the most trying circumstances. He promises never to leave us or forsake us.

Dr. Charles Stanley says, "We are not going to be able to smile every time trouble comes our way. In fact, there will be times when we wonder why some things happen. Yet when Christ is the center of your life, there is a peace deep inside that passes all understanding. There may be tears on your cheeks, but within there is a joy springing from the hope that God is in control."

Writing on the subject "Choose Hope," Morton Kelsey says he will never forget what happened to him when a bad crisis came. "I was terribly worried. Suddenly it came to me that it was just as easy to hope as to fear. As I switched over to hoping, almost immediately new springs of life bubbled up within me, carrying me through the crisis with greater peace and strength, if not with joy. The worst finally happened, but I was so sustained that I was able to walk on through."

Dr. Stanley says, "The Christian life is not a matter of pumping up something that is not within us, not trying to be like something we can never be. It is allowing the person of Jesus Christ, who lives within us, to flow His life through us by the power of the Holy Spirit."

So let us say with Jeremiah, "The LORD is my inheritance; therefore, I will hope in him! The LORD is wonderfully good to those who wait for him and seek him" (Lamentations 3:24 NLT).

THIRTY-FIVE

When Praising Is Difficult

Praise the LORD, for the LORD is good;
sing praise to his name, for that is pleasant.

—PSALM 135:3

⌒

God delights in our praise. He longs to bless us through our worship and praise. Yet we often find it difficult to praise Him, especially when life is not going as we think it should. God asks us to praise Him not because He needs to be "built up" but in order that He may bless us.

Jack Hayford says praising God through the Psalms will change us. Praising Him will aid in transforming us into the likeness of God. David said, "Praise the LORD, I tell myself; with my whole heart I will praise his holy name. Praise the LORD, I tell myself, and never forget the good things he does for me" (Psalm 103:1,2 NLT).

Yet David experienced times of trouble when he felt forsaken by God. On one such occasion he cried, "Save me, O God, for the waters have come up to my neck. I sink in the miry depths, where there is no foothold. I have come into the deep waters; the floods engulf me. I am worn out calling for help; my throat is parched. My eyes fail, looking for my God" (Psalm 69:1-3).

But a study of the Psalms will show us that David quickly bounced back from his feelings of dismay. We learn from him that praise can come out of our moments of pain and disappointment as well as out of our moments of joy and jubilation.

David says, "Come, let us bow down in worship, let us kneel before the LORD our Maker; for he is our God and we are the people of his pasture, the flock under his care. . . . Every day I will praise you and extol your name for ever and ever" (Psalm 95:6,7; 145:2).

Abraham also was a man who discovered the rewards of worship. On one occasion after he had worshiped the Lord, "the word of the LORD came to Abram in a vision: 'Do not be afraid, Abram. I am your shield, your very great reward'" (Genesis 15:1). Abraham received the greatest reward possible—the Lord Himself. After that, Abraham knew that he need never be afraid of the Lord. He knew that whatever happened, God had his best interest at heart.

We need never feel that everything has to be going without any trials or difficulties in order for us to praise God. We can sing and praise for joy because we know that God will work out every situation for our highest good.

Non-Christians and nominal Christians would think it senseless to praise God in the midst of difficulty. But in the midst of all kinds of trials the apostle Paul trusted in God and praised Him.

He wrote to the church at Rome: "I urge you, brothers, in view of God's mercy, to offer your bodies as living sacrifices, holy and pleasing to God—this is your spiritual act of worship. Do not conform any longer to the pattern of this world, but be transformed by the renewing of your mind. Then you will be able to test and approve what God's will is—his good, pleasing and perfect will" (Romans 12:1,2).

Paul would not have advised us to do anything that he himself did not practice. To offer our bodies as living sacrifices includes praising God regardless of circumstances. We notice that Paul says, "This is your spiritual act of worship." Of course, pleasing God and being in His perfect will encompasses praise. The pattern of this world is to ignore God's desire for praise and adoration and refuse to humble itself before God.

The psalmist said, "Great is the LORD and most worthy of praise; his greatness no one can fathom" (Psalm 145:3). How true! God indeed deserves our praise.

Fanny J. Crosby expressed that truth when she wrote the hymn "Praise Him! Praise Him!" Let's look at her first stanza and the chorus:

> Praise Him, praise Him!
> Jesus our blessed Redeemer!
> Sing, O earth, His wonderful love proclaim.
> Hail Him, hail Him! Highest archangels in glory;
> Strength and honor give to His holy name.
> Like a shepherd Jesus will guard His children;
> In His arms He carries them all day long.
> Praise Him, praise Him!
> Tell of His excellent greatness!
> Praise Him, praise Him! Ever in joyful song!

THIRTY-SIX

When You Feel Insecure

How great is the love the Father has lavished on us,
that we should be called children of God!
And that is what we are!

—1 JOHN 3:1

Knowing that God loves us so much that He calls us His children, how can we feel insecure? "It's about time you had the joy of discovering the truth about yourself," says Dr. Kevin Leman in his book *Measuring Up*—"that you have everything you need to come out a winner in this game called life." We were created to be the object of God's affections.

The forces of darkness are against us. We need to remember that the light of the Lord is greater than the darkness that surrounds us. If we belong to Christ, our feelings of insecurity do not come from Him. Usually our insecure feelings come from the messages given by the overall personalities and expressions of other people toward us as we were growing up. But as we "grow up" in the Spirit, we can learn to put away those feelings.

Paul tells us "to put off your old self" (Ephesians 4:22). We grow in our understanding that God knows and cares about our feelings of insecurity and wants to heal us.

Dr. David A. Seamands says in his book *Healing Grace,* "The first step in our healing is to realize that God understands where the feelings are coming from and is as brokenhearted about it as we are. He wants to work with us in freeing us from them, for He doesn't want His children despising themselves. Truly our only hope is a whole new way of viewing ourselves through the eyes of grace."*

God takes great delight in lifting us up and helping us to feel secure about ourselves. We must understand that our sense of being secure does not come from anything we do from the outside. It has to come from the inside as we change our attitudes and see ourselves as God sees us.

When Jesus died on the cross, He suffered not only for our sins but also for our pains. He now invites us to relinquish all our hurts to Him. His love and forgiveness alone can free us from our self-destructive feelings.

We may need help from a pastor or understanding godly friend. Our healing of insecurity is unlikely to come overnight. Those feelings didn't come to us overnight. But we can stop feeding on negative emotions and get a new sense of who we are—God's beloved children.

Paul said, "Let God transform you into a new person by changing the way you think. Then you will know what God wants you to do, and you will know how good and pleasing and perfect his will really is" (Romans 12:2 NLT). It is certainly God's will for us to feel secure about ourselves, just as He does.

Dr. Seamands suggests that we may want to set aside a three-week period in which we concentrate on listening to

---

* © 1998 by Victor Books. Reprinted with permission.

the Holy Spirit as He reminds us of who we are. We need to trust His affirming voice, then think His thoughts about us after Him. Cooperation with the Holy Spirit is essential.

As we read our Bibles, let's look for God's promises and passages that encourage us. Some people with insecurity problems stop praying and reading the Bible altogether. They feel unworthy to call upon God. Having lost their sense of God as a personal, loving, forgiving heavenly Father, they feel unable to trust Him with their true feelings. God is waiting for His confused children to come to Him and express their innermost needs. He already knows all about them, but for our sakes we need to tell Him.

God not only saves and sanctifies us, but He longs to heal and transform us, making us aware that we are His. Our very breath comes from God. Luke reminds us that "in him we live and move and exist" (Acts 17:28 NLT).

God created us to be the object of His affections. His grace and mercy are greater than our human minds can fathom. Nineteenth-century Frederick Faber expresses the truth of God's mercy in his hymn "There's a Wideness in God's Mercy."

> There's a wideness in God's mercy,
> Like the wideness of the sea;
> There's a kindness in His justice,
> Which is more than liberty.
>
> There is welcome for the sinner,
> And more graces for the good;
> There is mercy with the Savior;
> There is healing in His blood.

Receiving such mercy and love from our heavenly Father, we need not continue nursing feelings of insecurity.

THIRTY-SEVEN

When You Feel Pessimistic

*Always be full of joy in the Lord. I say it
again—rejoice! . . . For I can do everything with the
help of Christ who gives me the strength I need.*

—PHILIPPIANS 4:4,13 NLT

⌒

aul makes it clear that we are to rejoice in
the Lord. A few verses later he adds that he
can do everything he needs to do with the
help of Christ. What the Lord told Paul about how to live
includes you and me.

When I feel pessimistic, I am not rejoicing in the Lord,
nor am I asking Him to help me to do the thing I most
need to do—overcome my pessimistic feelings. We do not
honor God or help ourselves when we give in to pessimism.

A life of pessimism sometimes comes as a result of fear
or guilt. If guilt is our problem, we need to find out
whether our guilt is real or imagined. If it is real, we can
confess any known sin and turn from it. If fear is our problem, we need to find the reason for our fear, and ask the

Lord to help us overcome it. Then we need to believe in Him and rest in Him. We can be set free through the blood of Jesus.

Maybe you need to improve your lifestyle, especially if you feel pressured. Learn to take life a little easier. Do you take time for yourself each day? In addition to working, take time to read something uplifting or inspirational; listen to your favorite music; pursue a hobby; or simply sit quietly and let your imagination take you to fanciful places. Are you getting enough exercise? Taking a walk is usually more conducive to overcoming pessimism than watching television.

Don't take yourself or your problems too seriously. Learn to laugh at yourself and your mistakes. I had to learn to do that. It didn't come easily or overnight. I had to work at it, but it was worth the effort.

Admit to yourself that you are pessimistic. Your emotions can make you feel miserable. It does no good to tell yourself that you shouldn't feel that way. Try to find the cause or causes of your pessimism and deal with them. You have the power to respond to them in a variety of ways.

In her article "Self-Control: a Fruit of the Spirit," Margaret West writes, "Even when our emotions threaten to gallop away with us, the Holy Spirit hovers over us. We can always invite the Spirit of Jesus into our lives to help us develop a positive expression of our emotions and to endow us with liberating self-control."

Our true source of wholeness is the Bible and prayer. Overcoming pessimism can be speeded up by seeing God in nature around us. God created the beauty of the earth for our enjoyment. Let's revel in it and thank God for it.

Pessimism often leads to self-pity, another destructive emotion. Christian freelance writer Dr. Kenny Waters says, "Self-pity can be overcome, even if we are wallowing deep within it, by a three-step process. The stages are recognition, repentance and action."

Pessimism comes from the evil one. This doesn't mean we necessarily sin by living with a pessimistic attitude, but it does mean that God can help us overcome it. Paul tells us, "No temptation has seized you except what is common to man. And God is faithful; he will not let you be tempted beyond what you can bear. But when you are tempted, he will also provide a way out so that you can stand up under it" (1 Corinthians 10:13). Simply reading such Scriptures is of little avail; we need to meditate on helpful Scriptures until we *feel* their truth.

We know that nothing is impossible with God. Some people live with pessimism because they have lost sight of their goals or the dreams God placed in their heart. Dare to dream about what you can do. Recall happy times from your past. Know that you can be happy again. If you feel that you've never known happiness, God can heal that situation and help you to become the person He created you to be—one who rejoices in Him.

Realize that what Paul wrote to the Romans applies to you too: "God works for the good of those who love him, who have been called according to his purpose" (Romans 8:28). If you have accepted Christ Jesus as your personal Savior, you have been called according to His purpose and can rejoice in Him.

THIRTY-EIGHT

When You're Weary

Come to me, all you who are weary and
burdened, and I will give you rest.

—MATTHEW 11:28

〜⌒〜

*A*s long as we live in our human bodies we
will grow weary—physically and emotionally—from time to time. But for us to
experience constant weariness has never been God's
intention. Jesus said, "Take my yoke upon you and learn
from me, for I am gentle and humble in heart, and you will
find rest for your souls" (Matthew 11:29).

Even powerful servants of God can become weary.
Elijah was such a man. After he had called down fire from
heaven to lick up the water in the trenches to show that
God and not Baal was the all-powerful One, he received
news that Jezebel was out to destroy his life. Elijah was
afraid and ran for his life. At the end of the day he sat
down under a tree and prayed to die. Elijah had become
weary in body and soul. He was discouraged and worn-out
from his recent tasks and from Jezebel's threats.

Job became exceedingly weary from the sufferings he
experienced. He said, "My soul is weary of my life; I will

leave my complaint upon myself; I will speak in the bitterness of my soul" (Job 10:1 KJV).

The psalmist David often became weary because of his trials. At one point he said, "I am weary with my groaning; all night I make my bed swim; I drench my couch with my tears" (Psalm 6:6 NKJV). But David never allowed himself to feel that way for an extended time. He knew that God was his helper and deliverer.

The writer of the book of Hebrews knew our proneness to become weary, and he expressed our need to look only to Jesus. He wrote, "Think about all he [Jesus] endured when sinful people did such terrible things to him, so that you don't become weary and give up" (Hebrews 12:3 NLT). Turning our eyes upon Jesus and meditating on Him helps us to overcome our weariness.

In Paul's missionary journeys he often became weary. He wrote, "I have lived with weariness and pain and sleepless nights. Often I have been hungry and thirsty and have gone without food. Often I have shivered with cold, without enough clothing to keep me warm" (2 Corinthians 11:27 NLT). But Paul never allowed his weariness to stop him in his service to the Lord. When he was falsely accused for preaching the gospel, he knew he was innocent. He refused to accept false guilt that others tried to lay on him.

Those who experience weariness in God's service are often accused falsely. Dr. Robert A. Brimmer says, "Because false guilt always hampers productiveness, decreases self-value, destroys hope and consequently decreases a Christian's ability to serve the Lord, false guilt is a subtle but effective tool of the devil."

We can be assured that the Lord understands us and is present with us in our times of weariness. The writer to the Hebrews said, "Therefore, since we have a great high priest who has gone through the heavens, Jesus the Son of God, let us hold firmly to the faith we profess. For we do not have a high priest who is unable to sympathize with our weaknesses, but we have one who has been tempted in every way, just as we are—yet was without sin" (Hebrews 4:14,15).

The hymn "Tell It to Jesus" reminds us that when we become weary, we can experience relief by telling our troubles to Jesus. His first verse proclaims Jesus as our friend who can help:

Are you weary, are you heavy-hearted?
Tell it to Jesus, tell it to Jesus;
Are you grieving over joys departed?
Tell it to Jesus alone.
Tell it to Jesus, tell it to Jesus,
He is a friend that's well-known;
You have no other such a friend or brother,
Tell it to Jesus alone.

THIRTY-NINE

When You Have Trouble Meditating

Oh, how I love your law!
I meditate on it all day long.

—PSALM 119:97

⁓

Pagan meditation has caused many Christians to back away from biblical meditation. Biblical meditation is thinking on the Scriptures or concentrating on the Word of God in order to know God better. When we meditate we are not simply reading or studying the Bible, but allowing the Word of God to penetrate our hearts. Dr. Charles Stanley says that meditation is the most essential exercise we can engage in. The most important reason for meditation is to know God intimately.

A yogi told Rev. Malcolm Smith that he meditates to achieve union with God. Reverend Smith replied, "Christians meditate because we *have* union with God." As Christians we already have union with God, but meditation helps us to know Him better, to see Him as He is, and to view ourselves as God wants us to. Meditation is a God-given privilege that enables us to mature.

Andrew Murray, author of 240 books, wrote that in order to meditate, we must take time. "Give God time to reveal Himself to you. Give yourself time to be silent and quiet before Him, waiting to receive through the Spirit the assurance of His presence with you, His power working in you.

"Take time to read His Word as in His presence, that from it you may know what He asks of you and what He promises you." The busy father of nine children and founder of a seminary, Andrew Murray took time every day to meditate.

Meditation is not something to be done occasionally, but daily. David said of the follower of the Lord, "His delight is in the law of the LORD, and on his law he meditates day and night" (Psalm 1:2).

When Joshua was ready to lead the Israelites out of Egypt into their Promised Land, the Lord said to him: "Study this Book of the Law continually. Meditate on it day and night so you may be sure to obey all that is written in it. Only then will you succeed" (Joshua 1:8 NLT). We notice that the Lord told Joshua that the only way he could succeed was to meditate on the Word day and night.

Of course, to meditate on the Word we must know what it says. Dr. J.I. Packer says, "If I were the devil, one of my first aims would be to stop folk from reading the Bible." R. Kent Hughes says in his book *Disciplines of a Godly Man*, "We may be challenged, convicted and exhilarated with the call to meditation. The question is, How is this to be done? . . . Ideally we are to make meditation a part of our regular devotion, giving hidden time to reverently muttering [speaking to ourselves] God's Word."

Meditation on the Word quiets our spirits, increases our faith, and expands our view of God. Solomon wrote, "Tune your ears to wisdom, and concentrate on understanding. Cry out for insight and understanding. Search for them as you would for lost money or hidden treasure. Then you will understand what it means to fear the LORD, and you will gain knowledge of God" (Proverbs 2-5 NLT).

Even with all our knowledge of and need for meditation, it doesn't come easy for most of us, especially if we are new in the faith. But as we learn to meditate daily, we find that our hurried feelings are replaced by a quiet confidence that God is ever-present with us.

Personally, I find the best time for meditation is early in the morning before the tasks of the day consume my attention. I begin by thanking God for His love and goodness. Then I read my Bible and a devotional or two from an inspirational book. Many of the Psalms are good places to start. I mark the verses I find most helpful. For a period of time, I read and meditated on Psalm 91 every day. Choose Scriptures that are meaningful to you.

It's never too late to begin a more satisfying Christian life, a life that is anchored in our loving God and His Word.

FORTY

When You Feel Helpless

We wait in hope for the LORD;
he is our help and our shield.

—PSALM 33:20

～～⊃

All of us sometimes feel helpless—as if we can't accomplish the task at hand or an undertaking facing us in the future. Or maybe it's a situation we would like to change but feel helpless to do so. More than once the psalmist felt that way, but he knew his source of help. He said, "God is our refuge and strength, an ever-present help in trouble" (Psalm 46:1).

Over and over in Scripture we are reminded that the Lord is our helper when we feel helpless. The Lord, speaking through Isaiah, said, "Do not fear, for I am with you; do not be dismayed, for I am your God. I will strengthen you and help you; I will uphold you with my righteous right hand. . . . For I am the LORD, your God, who takes hold of your right hand and says to you, Do not fear; I will help you" (Isaiah 41:10,13).

The apostle Paul knew his helplessness, but, like the psalmist, he knew his source of help. He said, "When I am

161

weak, then I am strong" (2 Corinthians 12:10). Paul knew that he himself was helpless, but he also knew that in Christ he was strong. That is, with Christ indwelling him, his weakness became strength. The same can be true for you and me when we realize that Christ indwells us and will be our strength.

The feeling of helplessness creates in us strong negative emotions which can keep us spiritually defeated. Sometimes we feel helpless because we have undertaken a task that God never meant for us to assume. Are you feeling helpless because you're trying to accomplish too much? Have you set unrealistic goals for yourself?

Are you trying to imitate somebody else instead of being the individual God created you to be? That can give you a feeling of helplessness; you're trying to do or be what you're not supposed to be. Accept yourself and your own personality type, with the gifts and talents God gave you. God wants you to be yourself. He loves and accepts you as you are. Can you accept yourself as God does?

Are you a perfectionist who feels helpless because you are unable to keep everything in your house perfect? We sometimes feel helpless simply because we're so overburdened that we forget to take time for ourselves or to be still before God. Allow yourself to be human, not superhuman. God wants us to trust Him without feeling that we must be perfect in every area of life. Above all else, God wants us to know He loves us. His love permeates our very being.

If we were always self-reliant, feeling sufficient in ourselves, we would not need God's love and grace. Any good that we do is not to earn God's grace or approval. His grace is a free gift. Our good works are our response to God's love.

Let's say with David, "The LORD is my light and my salvation—whom shall I fear? The LORD is the stronghold of my life—of whom shall I be afraid?" (Psalm 27:1).

Shortly before his death, Pastor Henry Francis Lyte penned this hymn, showing that God is the One who is the helper of the helpless. Let's consider his first and fourth stanzas.

ABIDE WITH ME

Abide with me—fast falls the eventide;
The darkness deepens; Lord, with me abide!
When other helpers fail and comforts flee,
Help of the helpless, O abide with me.

Hold Thou Thy cross before my closing eyes;
Shine tho' the gloom and point me to the skies;
Heav'n's morning breaks and earth's
vain shadows flee;
In life, in death, O Lord, abide with me.

FORTY-ONE

When You Doubt Your Salvation

Salvation is found in no one else,
for there is no other name under heaven
given to men by which we must be saved.

—ACTS 4:12

⟋⟍⟋⟋⟋

Our salvation is not a matter of our feelings or of anything we do. It is a free gift from God. Our part is simply to repent, believe in Jesus, and accept His salvation. In his letter to Titus, Paul wrote, "[Christ] saved us, not because of righteous things we had done, but because of his mercy. He saved us through the washing of rebirth and renewal by the Holy Spirit' (Titus 3:5). When we are saved, we are made clean through the blood of Jesus.

Many Christians doubt their salvation and feel unworthy to call upon God. Yet God waits with open arms for them to hand their doubts over to Him and return to their original trust in Him. The enemy of our soul constantly seeks to fill us with doubt and thus make us miserable.

We can put Satan to flight by following Paul's admonition to "put on the full armor of God so that you can take your stand against the devil's schemes. . . . In addition to all this, take up the shield of faith, with which you can extinguish all the flaming arrows of the evil one" (Ephesians 6:11,16).

The well-known author Hannah Whitall Smith said she used to wake up in the morning to find a "perfect army of doubts clamoring" at her door for admittance. But she said she "made a pledge against doubting." She learned she could put on the shield of faith and hand over her doubts to God.

Are you doubting your salvation because you feel you have not measured up? God doesn't say anything about our need to measure up. The Word tells us, "If we confess our sins, he is faithful and just and will forgive us our sins and purify us from all unrighteousness" (1 John 1:9). God is a God of love and justice. He wants His children to trust Him, knowing He accepts us as we are and stands ready to forgive us when we ask.

Why could Paul preach the gospel with such great confidence? He said, "I am not ashamed of the gospel, because it is the power of God for the salvation of everyone who believes" (Romans 1:16). Have you believed in the Lord? Have you surrendered yourself to Him? That's all He asks of you.

Paul wrote to the Christians in Rome, "If you confess with your mouth, 'Jesus is Lord,' and believe in your heart that God raised him from the dead, you will be saved. For it is with your heart that you believe and are justified, and it is with your mouth that you confess and are saved" (Romans 10:9,10). What was true for the Romans is true for you and me as well.

There is saving power in the blood of Jesus. Paul wrote, "For our gospel did not come to you in word only, but also in power, and in the Holy Spirit and in much assurance" (1 Thessalonians 1:5 NKJV). The Lord wants us to be aware of that power which saves us and keeps us under His protective wing. In times of doubt, God's greatness is our source of comfort. He is the all-powerful, unchanging One whose love for us never ceases.

"When the enemy comes in like a flood, The Spirit of the LORD will lift up a standard against him" (Isaiah 59:19 NKJV).

So join in singing the second verse of Jack P. Scholfield's hymn "Saved, Saved."

> He saves me from every sin and harm,
> Secures my soul each day;
> I'm leaning strong on His mighty arm,
> I know He'll guide me all the way.
> Saved by His power divine,
> Saved to new life sublime!
> Life now is sweet and my joy is complete,
> For I'm saved, saved, saved!

FORTY-TWO

When You Doubt God's Blessings

Victory comes from you, O LORD.
May your blessings rest on your people.

—PSALM 3:8 NLT

⌒

Many of God's children have experiences that cause them to doubt God's blessings. When sickness lingers, death occurs, or disaster strikes, they wonder why. Does God care, or has He withdrawn His love and blessings?

Even the psalmist cried out, "My God, my God, why have you forsaken me? Why are you so far from saving me, so far from the words of my groaning?" (Psalm 22:1). But later he said, "No one whose hope is in you will ever be put to shame. . . . All the ways of the LORD are loving and faithful for those who keep the demands of his covenant" (Psalm 25:3,10).

Do you suppose Daniel felt God's blessings when he was about to be thrown into the lions' den? I doubt if he did. But God sent an angel to lock the lions' mouths, and Daniel came out unharmed.

Was Job aware of God's blessings when Satan had permission to take him through all kinds of evil? No, but eventually Job won the victory and his trials ended. "The LORD blessed the latter part of Job's life more than the first" (Job 42:12). Job ended up receiving more blessings than he could ever have imagined.

If you look at the underside of a tapestry, you may see a lot of loose ends or rough spots. That's the way life sometimes looks from our viewpoint. But if we look at the other side, we'll see a beautifully woven work. If we look only at the ugly things coming our way, we may doubt God's blessings. But if we view them from God's perspective, we'll know that God is still in charge and that He can use everything in life to bless us. Difficulties may blind our spiritual eyes to God's love and faithfulness.

Charles Stanley says, "God has a purpose for each situation we face. He also has a plan that leads to hope when we learn to trust Him for the outcome of our circumstances."

"'I know the plans I have for you,' says the LORD. 'They are plans for good and not for disaster, to give you a future and a hope'" (Jeremiah 29:11 NLT). Those plans include God's blessings. You are important to God, and He wants to free you from doubt.

When you doubt God's blessings, open your Bible and find His promises to bless you. Meditate on those promises and know they are for you. Here are a few you might like to start with.

"Blessed are all who take refuge in him. . . . For the LORD God is a sun and shield; the LORD bestows favor and honor; no good thing does he withhold from those whose walk is blameless. O LORD Almighty, blessed is the man who trusts in you" (Psalm 2:12; 84:11-12).

"See, I am setting before you today a blessing and a curse—the blessing if you obey the commands of the LORD your God that I am giving you today" (Deuteronomy 11:26,27).

"Blessed is the man who does not walk in the counsel of the wicked or stand in the way of sinners or sit in the seat of mockers" (Psalm 1:1).

"Blessed are those who have learned to acclaim you, who walk in the light of your presence, O LORD. . . . Blessed is the man who fears the LORD, who finds great delight in his commands" (Psalm 89:15; 112:1).

"A faithful man will be richly blessed" (Proverbs 28:20).

"To this you were called so that you may inherit a blessing" (1 Peter 3:9).

You'll probably be surprised to find many more of God's promises to bless you. Underline them. Return to them again and again.

If you still doubt God's promises, take a look at the second stanza of R. Kelso Carter's favorite old hymn.

STANDING ON THE PROMISES

Standing on the promises that cannot fail,
When the howling storms of doubt and fear assail,
By the living Word of God I shall prevail,
Standing on the promises of God.
Standing, standing,
Standing on the promises of God my Savior;
Standing, standing,
I'm standing on the promises of God.

FORTY-THREE

When You Feel Downcast

Why are you downcast, O my soul?
Why so disturbed within me?
Put your hope in God,
for I will yet praise him,
my Savior and my God.

—PSALM 42:5

⎯⎯⎯⎯⎯⎯

*D*avid talks to his soul and asks, "Why are you downcast?" Do you ever ask yourself that question? Most of us have asked similar questions. David knew that God was his hope, but he still had times of feeling downcast. Yet he knew where to turn for help. He realized that God could lift him out of his pit of despair.

On another occasion the psalmist assures us, "If the LORD delights in a man's way, he makes his steps firm; though he stumble, he will not fall, for the LORD upholds him with his hand" (Psalm 37:23,24).

David says, "Surely, O LORD, you bless the righteous; you surround them with your favor as with a shield" (Psalm 5:12). Regardless of our feelings, the Lord is present to bless us. He will lift us up and bring us out of our worst feelings. We can do as David did when he said, "In the morning I lay my requests before you and wait in expectation" (Psalm 5:3). We notice David said he waited *in expectation*. When we wait in expectation, we stop being anxious before the answer comes.

Again David spoke words of hope: "Those who know your name will trust in you, for you, LORD, have never forsaken those who seek you. . . . You hear, O LORD, the desire of the afflicted; you encourage them, and you listen to their cry" (Psalm 9:10; 10:17). Being downcast is a form of being afflicted. God hears and answers. "You give me your shield of victory, and your right hand sustains me" (Psalm 18:35).

Referring to the Lord, Isaiah offers these encouraging words: "You come to the help of those who gladly do right, who remember your ways" (Isaiah 64:5).

Paul experienced many times when he felt downcast. "We are hard pressed on every side, but not crushed; perplexed, but not in despair; persecuted, but not abandoned; struck down, but not destroyed" (2 Corinthians 4:8-9). But like David, Paul never allowed his feelings to rule. He knew where to turn for comfort. He said, "But God, who comforts the downcast, comforted us" (2 Corinthians 7:6).

One of the paradoxes of the Christian faith is that we *grow* through such difficulties as feeling downcast. As Bernard Baruch said, "The art of living lies not in eliminating but in growing with troubles." That statement is hard for us to accept. And it can hardly be true for us unless we put our trust in God and know that He will be with us.

I don't know who spoke the following words, but I see them as truth. "For the Christian, disappointments are opportunities to learn more of Christ and His will for our lives. And it is in our disappointments that we learn to live out the truth spoken by Paul, 'All things work together for our good.'" Even when you're downcast, God can turn that around and make your situation work out for your good.

Minister/author Devern Fromke said, "There is no pain, no suffering, no frustration, no disappointment that cannot be cured or taken up and used for higher ends. . . . You can react in self-pity and in frustration, or you can respond with confidence and courage, allowing the pressure to make you better." Our part is to surrender those problems to the Lord. He is more concerned about our troubles than we are. And He is the One who can lift us out of our downcast feelings.

FORTY-FOUR

When You're Wandering in a Valley

Even when I walk through the dark valley of death,
I will not be afraid, for you are close beside me.
Your rod and your staff protect and comfort me.

—PSALM 23:4 NLT

⌒

We are not often called upon to walk through the valley of death, but most of us have experienced times when we felt as if we were stumbling around in some kind of valley. It may be a valley of disappointment, indecision, waiting, despair, loneliness, pain (either physical or emotional), or some other type of valley.

But regardless of the kind of valley, we can say with the psalmist, "You are close beside me." The Lord will comfort us and not leave us too long in a valley, but will lead us safely through.

Do you feel as if you're having to walk through a dry, desolate valley? David said, "He [God] sends the springs into the valleys, which flow among the hills" (Psalm 104:10 NKJV). God will send water into our dry valleys and console us. He knows how dry we feel and how dry our path, and He will send relief.

Do you find your valley so dark that you can hardly see ahead? David said, "You will light my lamp; The LORD my God will enlighten my darkness" (Psalm 18:28 NKJV). In His time, you will see His light shining upon you, turning your darkness into light.

Elijah went through such a hopeless-looking valley that he prayed for God to take his life. But God manifested His patience with Elijah. He wasn't ready to take Elijah home. There was still work for him to do. God showed Elijah that, contrary to his belief, he was not alone in his dedication.

In Elijah's feeling of being alone in a valley, God let him know there were many other faithful ones. Elijah was not to bask in misery and self-pity, but to get back into action. When we're in a valley of despondency, maybe we need simply to find something to do in God's service.

William Cushing, a nineteenth-century preacher, must have felt as if he were wandering in a valley when, before he was 50 years old, he lost his voice. He wondered how God could use him. But after that, he wrote more than 300 hymns. Though he could not speak audibly, God multiplied his words to bless generations to come. One of his hymns is "Under His Wings." Let's look at his first stanza and chorus:

Under His wings I am safely abiding,
Though the night deepens and tempests are wild;
Still I can trust Him—I know He will keep me;
He has redeemed me and I am His child.

Under His wings, under His wings,
Who from His love can sever?
Under His wings my soul shall abide,
Safely abide forever.

FORTY-FIVE

When You Need Comfort

*Praise be to the God and Father of our Lord Jesus Christ,
the Father of compassion and the God of all comfort,
who comforts us in all our troubles.*

—2 CORINTHIANS 1:3,4

⟋⟍⟋⟍

Many people think "the God of all comfort" is the loveliest of all the names that reveal God. I agree. *All* comfort means every kind of comfort; no circumstance is excluded. Whatever your problems, anxieties, or hurts, God is your comfort.

God doesn't ask if you are *worthy* of comfort. He calls us worthy because we belong to Christ (if we have trusted Him for salvation). God is never indifferent to our trials. He knows, cares, and comforts. *The God of all comfort* is not simply a pious, meaningless phrase. It is genuine comfort that enfolds all of life's trials.

The Lord said through Isaiah, "As a mother comforts her child, so will I comfort you" (Isaiah 66:13). A good mother never fails to comfort her child when he needs comfort. God, who is so much more loving and caring than the best mother, will not fail to comfort you. The psalmist, who so often needed comfort, said, "You, O LORD, have helped me and comforted me" (Psalm 86:17).

Speaking through Jeremiah, God said, "I have loved you with an everlasting love; I have drawn you with loving-kindness. . . . I will turn their mourning into gladness; I will give them comfort and joy instead of sorrow" (Jeremiah 31:3,13).

Hannah Whitall Smith said, "Strangely enough . . . it is easy for us when we are happy and do not need comforting to believe that our God is the 'God of all comfort,' but as soon as we are in trouble and need it, it seems impossible to believe that there could be any comfort for us anywhere." We forget that Jesus said, "Blessed are those who mourn, for they will be comforted" (Matthew 5:4).

Early in His ministry Jesus proclaimed, "The Spirit of the Lord is upon me, for he has appointed me to preach Good News to the poor. He has sent me to proclaim that captives will be released, that the blind will see, that the downtrodden will be freed from their oppressors, and that the time of the Lord's favor has come" (Luke 4:18,19 NLT). In other words, Jesus is saying, "Whatever your problem, I am here to comfort you." Our Comforter is not far away. He *abides* with us forever.

Just before Jesus left this earth and ascended to heaven, He told His disciples, "I will pray the Father, and he shall give you another Comforter, that he may abide with you forever" (John 14:16 KJV). The Comforter does not come and go. He is always present with us when we need Him.

Jesus also said, "Peace I leave with you; my peace I give you. . . . Do not let your hearts be troubled and do not be afraid" (John 14:27). Jesus is our Comforter who gives us peace and tells us not to be afraid. Jesus told His disciples that He would bless those in sorrow.

When we need comfort, the indwelling Comforter brings to our minds comforting facts we have read about our Lord. He may bring to our remembrance a Scripture verse we have read, the verse of a comforting hymn, or some comforting thought about the Lord and His care. Instead of listening to the voice of despair or the voice of the evil one, we can listen to the voice of the Comforter.

The psalmist often experienced various kinds of sorrow, and he needed the comfort of the Lord. He said, "In the multitude of my anxieties within me, Your comforts delight my soul" (Psalm 94:19 NKJV). The Lord's comforts can also delight your soul as you pour out your troubles and anxieties to Him. Hannah Whitall Smith said, "If we are to be comforted, we must make up our minds to believe every single solitary word of comfort God has ever spoken; and we must refuse utterly to listen to any words of discomfort spoken by our own hearts, or by our circumstances." She said that whoever will adopt this plan "will come, sooner or later, into a state of abounding comfort."

It is the Lord's desire that His people receive His comfort. He spoke through Isaiah saying, "Comfort, comfort my people, says your God" (Isaiah 40:1).

Inspired by those words, seventeenth-century Johannes Olearius composed the hymn "Comfort, Comfort Ye My People." His first stanza says:

> Comfort, comfort ye my people,
> Seek ye peace, thus saith our God;
> Comfort those who sit in darkness,
> Mourning 'neath their sorrow's load.
> Speak ye to Jerusalem
> Of the peace that waits for them;
> Tell her that her sins I cover,
> And her warfare now is over.

FORTY-SIX

When You Don't Feel Like Singing

Sing joyfully to the LORD, you righteous; it is fitting for the upright to praise him. Praise the LORD with the harp; make music to him on the ten-stringed lyre. Sing to him a new song; play skillfully, and shout for joy.

—PSALM 33:1-3

Worship and praise include singing. Throughout the Scriptures we are told to praise the Lord with singing. Nowhere does the Bible say we are to sing and praise only when we feel like it. We are to sing even if our heart is broken.

Why should we worship and praise? The psalmist says, "Come, let us bow down in worship, let us kneel before the LORD our Maker; for he is our God and we are the people of his pasture, the flock under his care" (Psalm 95:6,7). God desires and deserves our praise because "he is our God and we are the people of his care."

It should be perfectly natural for us to praise the One who made us, who gives us life, and who loves us so much. Unfortunately, many people give little thought to the fact that we belong to God and that He is worthy of our praise in song. The psalmist says, "Whoever offers praise glorifies Me" (Psalm 50:23 NKJV).

Jack Hayford says, "It seems that in worship, God is wanting to meet us and pour His beauty and His holiness into our lives." Our singing not only brings glory to God but also allows His beauty to become a part of our lives.

Paul said, "Speak to one another with psalms, hymns and spiritual songs. Sing and make music in your heart to the Lord" (Ephesians 5:19). You may say, "I don't have a musical voice." That makes no difference to God. He looks at your heart and your motives. God made your voice; it is beautiful to Him. He delights to hear you sing.

"Worship the LORD with gladness," said the psalmist; "come before him with joyful songs" (Psalm 100:2). At another time he said, "I will be glad and rejoice in you; I will sing praise to your name, O Most High" (Psalm 9:2). As you read the Psalms, you will discover that David kept his promise to sing praise to God. He praised God in every circumstance, the bad as well as the good.

When David was in the desert of Judah he sang, "Because your love is better than life, my lips will glorify you. I will praise you as long as I live, and in your name I will lift up my hands. . . . With singing lips my mouth will praise you" (Psalm 63:3-5). Singing is one way for us to express our devotion to God.

One of my earliest memories of my mother is her singing. She especially sang as she washed dishes and as she churned. You may never have lived in the country and don't know anything about churning cream to turn it into butter. And you may never have lived without an automatic dishwasher. Those chores took time for a mother of four. But such inconveniences (as we might call them today) never kept Mother from praising God in song.

Mother would have said with the psalmist David, "I will praise you, O LORD, with all my heart; I will tell of all your wonders. I will be glad and rejoice in you; I will sing praise to your name, O Most High" (Psalm 9:1,2). And with David she would have advised others, "Sing praises to God, sing praises; sing praises to our King, sing praises. . . . Sing to the LORD a new song, for he has done marvelous things" (Psalm 47:6; 98:1).

Probably no one has ever sung and praised God as much as David. He often made such declarations as: "My heart is steadfast, O God; I will sing and make music with all my soul. . . . I will praise you, O LORD, among the nations; I will sing of you among the peoples" (Psalm 108:1,3).

Not only did David himself sing to God, but he directed everybody and everything else to do likewise. "Shout with joy to God, all the earth! Sing the glory of his name; make his praise glorious! . . . Sing to God, sing praise to his name, extol him who rides on the clouds—his name is the LORD—and rejoice before him" (Psalm 66:1,2; 68:4).

Nineteenth-century Philip P. Bliss wrote the hymn "I Will Sing of My Redeemer." Many of us have sung it in our churches. Let's look at his last stanza.

I will sing of my Redeemer
And His heavenly love to me;
He from death to life hath brought me,
Son of God with Him to be.

FORTY-SEVEN

When You Fear the Enemy

*You, dear children, are from God and have
overcome them, because the one who is in you is
greater than the one who is in the world.*

—1 JOHN 4:4

〜〜〜

When we accept Christ as our personal
Savior, we have the Holy Spirit within
us. John assures us that He is "greater
than the one who is in the world." Jesus declares, "The
thief [Satan] comes only to steal and kill and destroy; I
have come that they may have life, and have it to the full"
(John 10:10). In light of those two statements, we can rest
in the knowledge that we need not fear the power of the
enemy. Jesus came to give us abundant life.

Of course we do have an enemy. Peter warns us, "Be
self-controlled and alert. Your enemy the devil prowls
around like a roaring lion looking for someone to devour"
(1 Peter 5:8). But if we are living in harmony with the will
of God, we have no reason to fear the enemy in our lives.
John tells us, "We know that anyone born of God does not
continue to sin; the one who was born of God keeps him
safe, and the evil one cannot harm him" (1 John 5:18).

Fear is one of Satan's favorite tools. Charles Stanley says fear can make us freeze in terror. Fear weakens us. If we yield to Satan's temptations and allow him to do so, he will bring us to feelings of doubt, fear, frustration, and all kinds of evil. That's why Peter said, "Be on the alert." Let's remember, too, that Satan is a liar. He tries to make us believe we are helpless and worthless.

This doesn't mean that everything that goes wrong in our lives is the work of the enemy. We live in an evil world, and many of our trials are simply the result of the world we live in. Some of the bad things that happen to us result from our own wrong decisions.

All of this shows why it is so important for us to stay in touch with God—reading His Word daily, talking with Him, living for Him, and being sure of our position in Christ: righteous in His sight.

God understands everything we face, and He will provide the strength to overcome the enemy. God invites us to trust Him even with the smallest detail of our lives. On our own, we cannot stand against the enemy. But through Christ, the victory is ours. He will empower us to overcome and to do God's will.

John wrote to his followers, "I write to you, young men, because you have overcome the evil one. . . . I write to you, young men, because you are strong, and the word of God lives in you, and you have overcome the evil one" (1 John 2:13,14). Confirming the words of John, Jesus said, "In this world you will have trouble. But take heart! I have overcome the world" (John 16:33). Paul wrote, "Do not be overcome by evil, but overcome evil with good" (Romans 12:21).

Paul also wrote, "Finally, be strong in the Lord and in his mighty power. Put on the full armor of God so that you can take your stand against the devil's schemes. For our struggle is not against flesh and blood, but against the rulers, against the authorities, against the powers of this dark world and against the spiritual forces of evil in the heavenly realms. Therefore put on the full armor of God, so that when the day of evil comes, you may be able to stand your ground, and after you have done everything, to stand" (Ephesians 6:10-13).

Many years before those words were spoken, the psalmist wrote, "Wait patiently for the LORD. Be brave and courageous. Yes, wait patiently for the LORD" (Psalm 27:14 NLT). Sometimes we may have to wait for the Lord to overcome the evil one for us. It also takes courage for us to stand against the evil one. But we must depend on the Lord.

We need not fear our spiritual enemy because the Lord is greater than he. "God has said, 'Never will I leave you; never will I forsake you.' So we say with confidence, 'The Lord is my helper; I will not be afraid'" (Hebrews 13:5,6).

The Hope of Love

Since God is love, there is no hope for our hearts except in His love. In the light of that truth, let's consider these words from Emmet Fox:

There is no difficulty that enough
love will not conquer;
No disease that enough love will not heal;
No door that enough love will not open;
No gulf that enough love will not bridge;
No wall that enough love will not throw down;
No sin that enough love will not redeem.

Other Books by
Marie Shropshire